Get on the Peace Train:

A Journey from Anger to Harmony

How do successful people cope with anger – their own and that of others?

A powerful and proven method to be happier, more successful, and more influential than you ever thought possible.

Lynn D. Johnson, Ph.D.

Copyright © 2004-2007 Lynn D. Johnson, Ph.D.

Printed in the United States of America

Third Edition

ISBN 0-9762734-0-3

This publication is designed to provide help for those who experience particular emotional problems but is not a substitute for competent professional help. You may need more help than this book can provide. Do not hesitate to seek the services of a medical or mental health professional.

Head Acre Publishing
166 East 5900 South, Ste. B-108
Salt Lake City, UT 84107-7273

As a reader of my book, you are entitled to updates. Please go to my website, http://drlynnjohnson.com. There you find my blog, free downloads, and sometimes even a free book to download. I'd be glad to have you visit.

A Note to the Reader

I have done two things in this book that sometimes confuse people. In this edition, I want to alert you about those.

First, I sometimes capitalize Anger. I do this to suggest something that may seem silly, namely that I am inviting you to think of anger as something outside of yourself. Think of some person in your past who tried to get you to do things that weren't in your best interest – throughout most of high school, for example! If you are a religious person, you can think of it as a devil who tries to get you to do the wrong thing, a temptation. So when I say, "Perhaps Anger is trying to convince you . . ." then you should think of anger as someone trying to talk to into something. I find that way of thinking about problems, even if it seems odd, helps people think more objectively about their own bad habits.

Second, when I use a typeface like this, it is to talk to people who are coping with angry folks. Whether it is your boss, your friend, or a close family member, some people read this book to get help in coping with anger in others. In the words of my friend John Lund, they are trying to learn how to hug a porcupine. When you see this, you know I am talking to people coping with anger in others.

Finally, for both those who want to control anger in their lives, and those who are coping, if you wish to get the very most out of this little book, *use a diary!* There is now abundant evidence that using a diary will help in many ways. You are more committed, you can track your progress, you can reflect on who you are and what your experiences teach you. You could read this book in an afternoon, but then you have not benefitted in the least. Use a diary.

Lynn Johnson

Contents

Introduction

Andrew was a senior vice president of a financial services firm. I was coaching him through a big transition in his workplace. The company he worked for, "ABC Financial" (not the real name, of course!) had been taken over, and a new president was flown in from Manhattan to increase profit. The new man, whom we will call George, relied on bluster and threats to "shape up the troops." He bragged about being a tough, mean boss who wouldn't take any excuses. George liked to rely on temper tantrums to motivate people, and he would blow up regularly.

Andrew was disheartened. He had loved his job before, and now he hated it. He hated the fact that his best people were trying madly to find new positions, positions where they wouldn't be pounced on and devoured by the boss. He hated his inability to protect his employees from George's tirades. He hated the constant pressure George put on him to do more with less, faster and better. He hated the fact that he hated to go to work.

Andrew had contacted me to help him through the transition, and while there were small suggestions that seemed to reduce his stress, the overall fact was that he was losing his spirit for his work. Like his subordinates, he was working on his resume, and dreaming of ways to escape. He was able to line up some opportunities, and began to feel less stressed. So I suggested an experiment.

Instead of leaving without really facing the angry boss, I proposed that Andrew think about what he would really like to say to George, if he had the chance. Can't you predict what he wanted to say? He wanted to rage at George, to accuse him of making the place impossible, he wanted to criticism him for running a great business into the ground. Anger tends to elicit more anger.

But sometimes there is something more profound behind the anger. "And behind that anger at George," I asked, "what do you feel that you cannot talk about?" Suddenly Andrew collapsed, his shoulder heaving. He was weeping, weeping for the loss, for the pain, and for the senselessness of it all. "Behind the anger . . . isn't there a great deal of sadness?" Andrew agreed.

We talked about the common strategy of responding to anger with more anger. It is completely understandable, but not at all useful, I suggested. Anger only begets more anger, and you are caught in a pointless spiral of aggression. How can we create a situation where each person can benefit, I asked? How can we make this win-win?

It cannot be done, Andrew maintained. George didn't respect anything but anger, he was sure. Any display of weakness would be a disaster.

But is it?

*   *   *   *   *   *   *

When I was getting my Ph.D. degree, we studied the various mental disorders, anxiety, depression, psychosis . . . we memorized diagnostic trees and practiced diagnostic interviews. Soon we could distinguish unipolar from bipolar depression, alcohol abuse from dependence, and dissociative identity disorder from Munchausen's syndrome.

When I began practicing as a psychologist, I discovered something quite alarming. Something had been left out! Anger was an emotional issue that caused my patients more problems than depression and anxiety. I had no training in it. What was worse was that in those days there seemed to be a sense of approval for people "expressing anger." The notion seemed to be that by acting angry, we would somehow be better communicators. There was even a psychologist who specialized in teaching people how to fight fair in marriage, how to "harness" anger in supposedly constructive ways.

That was not my own experience. I found that when I got angry at my wife, and tried to express that, things got worse rather than better. If I expressed anger at co-workers, the outcome was tension and anger coming right back at me. I wondered about my own profession. I wondered if we were rather foolish to think that anger was helpful.

It hasn't helped to see that over the years, nationally recognized marriage and family therapists, many personal friends of mine, have gotten divorced. We had sown winds of "openness and honesty, speaking up when angry" and now we were reaping the whirlwind.

Yet it is so easy to become angry. Why was that? I struggled to keep a cool head, to measure my responses and yet it was all so simple to just let go. I was amazed at how easily I – and others – seem to be able to be angry.

I found more and more people who were frightened and intimidated by angry people in their families, and I realized how anger was a bully's way, how one could get cheap power by throwing anger around.

Another thing I found was that the angry people were isolated and alone. They often seemed to think that if they simply showed enough anger, people would be sure to respect and care about them. Jealousy, accusations, criticism all drove people away, yet those who were jealous, accusing and critical seemed astounded when they ended up being avoided. Somehow they expected people around them to listen to their rage and yet love them.

At the same time, there was (and still is) an idea in feminism that anger was a good feeling, something that would help women take charge of their lives. There was a movement to help women by convincing them – the feminists said, enlightening them – that they were oppressed by a partriarical system. These feminists would angrily tell me that their anger helped and empowered them. They thought that anger had helped women obtain the vote in the early twentieth century, and it would help them again.

Never mind that my reading of history suggested the opposite, that anger had stymied the movement for votes for women, and that only a series of politically astute moves helped obtain their aim. Using the head, not the fist, helped women advance. Never mind that Martin Luther King, Jr., a man who accomplished so very much, was very clear that his disciples must not use anger. Never mind that Mahatma Gandhi (who was King's model) also refused to use anger.

I came to believe that anger doesn't help, *unless your aim is to destroy your opponent.* In this case, anger is very useful. If we have to go to war against someone, anger serves us well, but if we have to work with them, I saw that anger was very counterproductive.

It was not that I dislike these feminist sisters. I am sympathetic with their aims. Fairness is needed. I know full well that we men can be very demanding, very unfair, and insensitive. We can be jerks.

It is completely understandable that women would be angry with us. Some women had been terribly abused by bullies of husbands. No one could criticize anger in such cases.

The justification didn't bother me, but the results did. I began to believe that anger simply doesn't work. It is counterproductive and creates more problems than it solves. It seemed to me that anger made people more rigid, less intelligent . . . and less capable of having positive relationships. And frankly, anger causes as many problems when women use it as when men use anger. I learned that women are just as likely to hit their spouse as men are during arguments.

Anger is a classic case of the cure for a problem being far worse than the disease. There must be other ways of handling these problems, ways that avoided the Scylla and Charybdis (the fabled "rock and a hard place" of Greek mythology) of passive victimhood on the one hand and reaction-producing rage on the other. There has to be a better way.

And there is a better way! Thanks to breakthroughs in brain-scan technology, neurologists and psychologists began to learn how the brain actually worked, and what the effect of certain emotional states was on the brain's effectiveness. We discovered that there is very good reason that anger impairs the brain's abilities. We even began to discover how to improve the brain's tendency to be angry.

*   *   *   *   *   *   *

Andrew explored his options with the "new" ABC Corp. There weren't many for him. Mostly he saw himself leaving the company to pursue other career options. He wanted to get away, and formulated a plan to do that. Since he was about to leave anyway, I suggested he talk to George about his reactions to the changes in the company. I pointed out how anger begets anger, but behind that anger might be a way to talk to George. Perhaps if Andrew were to talk about how sad he was with the changes in the company, George's anger might not have anywhere to go! Well, Andrew thought, what do I have to lose?

He scheduled a meeting with George, and went in, determined to talk honestly about his vulnerable feelings of sadness, defeat, and his intention to leave the company. For the first time, Andrew saw a new side. George was not angry. If anything, George seemed paralyzed when Andrew didn't want to fight him. As he listened, a new side of him emerged. He was touched by Andrew's honesty and asked him how he could help. He said he wanted to save Andrew, keep him in the organization. Unfortunately for the company, it was too late. Andrew had already made his decision. They lost a valued employee.

*   *   *   *   *   *   *

Over the years I began to write brief thoughts about anger, usually after working with a couple, a business executive, or an individual whose anger was self-defeating. I used these little sheets as handouts as I worked with angry people. And every few months, I would realize something new, something I could add. Another sheet was the result. My single page handout became three, six, seven, eight pages long. It kept growing and growing. Every month or so I would add another page.

I was reminded of the very old Steve McQueen movie, *The Blob* where a package of lime gelatine from outer space takes over the world. My anger handout package was like The Blob, getting larger and larger. Yet so many patients, executives, and colleagues liked my anger handouts. They encouraged me to turn them into a small booklet, something that could be a resource for angry people. I realized at once that was 100% of the human race. I could see the value!

Originally I wrote this material for clients who had been overly controlled by their own anger. As time has gone on, I have added material for people who are influenced or intimidated by the anger of others.

So I have some words to say to those who have to cope with the anger of other people. Whether it is a spouse, a boss, or an acquaintance, we often have to deal with anger in others. I want to speak to you, too.

I believe there is a good deal we can do to improve our lives, and conquering anger is a great place to start, now is a great time, and you are a great person to make the start.

Lynn D. Johnson, Ph.D.
Salt Lake City, Utah
September 2004
http://drlynnjohnson.com

Chapter One

The Challenge of Anger

"Anger is an acid that can do more harm to the vessel in which it is stored than to anything on which it is poured.".
— Mark Twain

Perhaps anger is a practical joke that Mother Nature has played on the human race. In a primitive society, anger helps us survive. We can fight off aggressors or drive away bears or lions from our flocks with the energy that anger gives us. But in a civilized society, anger generally backfires and causes much trouble.

Have you ever been in trouble because of your own anger? Oh, I don't mean legal problems or something like that. People sometimes get arrested because of their anger, or, speaking more clearly, because of what they do when they are angry. That kind of trouble is pretty obvious. Just because this type of trouble isn't something you have faced, doesn't mean I am not talking to you.

I am talking about something more simple, more subtle. Have you ever done something while you were angry and then later wished you hadn't have done it? At the time it seemed to be the thing to do, did it not? The logic of the situation was overwhelming. Yet later you cool down. You look back. And you wonder, "What *was* I thinking?" How can something that seems so necessary at one time seem so short-sighted later?

To Anger is Human

We have all done this. The brain is wired in such a way that everyone experiences anger. Most of us have already figured out we were angry, we were short-sighted. The reason for this is very simple: When we are angry we are less intelligent.

The part of our brain that directs anger is called the "reptile brain." Perhaps it will help you to understand a bit about how your brain works. This reptile brain is a small area at the core of the brain, the most primitive part. If you were to look at a picture of the brain of an alligator and then look at a picture of our own reptile brain, you would notice that they look just alike.

Peek at the Working Brain

Biologists sometimes say we have an angel, a monkey, and a lizard living inside our heads all the time. Why do they say that? What does it mean to how we live our lives?

Since the invention of machines that can actually look at the working brain, like the PET scan and the Functional MRI (fMRI), neurologists and psychologists have learned a tremendous amount about how the brain actually operates. The three major areas of the brain, the reptile brain (thalamus and brain stem), the mammal brain (monkey brain, the limbic system) and the angel brain (neocortex, the highest brain, or human brain) all operate together. Every part is necessary.

The highest brain allows us to plan and perform complicated physical tasks, analyze complex problems, speak and understand languages, dream, hope, believe, and grow. This cortex is divided up into areas that have specialities, but that doesn't concern us in this book. Instead we will emphasize one thing: this part of the brain is wonderful at problem-solving, judging, deciding, and planning. When the cortex is energized and operating, we make better decisions.

Underneath that we have the limbic system, the emotional brain. I like to think of a troop of monkeys when I think of the limbic system. They operate on emotion, the speciality of the limbic system. Your instinctive emotions of anger, fear, and despair are all experienced in that monkey brain. Also, positive emotions such as love and curiosity are focused there.

And what about the reptile brain underneath that? That part of our brain is vital. When we are under attack, there is a quiet self-preservation mode that comes into play. The reptile brain becomes dominant. It gives us the energy to fight our enemies. Your behavior is driven by primitive instincts. The higher brain is quiet, on the sidelines. What we say and do is motivated by the primitive instincts. If we were fighting for our life, this primitive behavior might just save our life.

But there is a cost to letting the reptile brain be the driver. We lose our ability to think clearly and intelligently. And in a modern society, thinking clearly is vital.

The reptile brain makes us want to *do something* when we are angry. It is a brain of action, not thinking. While anger helped our ancestors survive, today it makes it very hard for us to flourish and profit. Just because it is a natural feeling, wired into us, doesn't mean that we have to be controlled by it now. I suggest that we <u>can</u> challenge anger. We <u>can</u> set our goal to be more calm, intelligent, and effective. We <u>can</u> decide to not let anger control us.

The Reptile Brain

Let's look at that a bit further. There are certainly bad moods such as anger or anxiety that reduce our performance. We now know that when we are in those bad moods, that primitive part of our brain is more "in charge."

So when you are upset, your reptile brain is most energized, and your higher brain functions are more quiet. They are being driven by your mood. Have you noticed that when you are in a bad mood, you say and do the same old things and you aren't very creative? That lack of creativity is a sure sign the reptile brain is mainly in control of your behavior.

When the alligator brain is calling the shots, the rest of the brain seems to "step back" and becomes less active. On brain activity tests of angry people (PET scans, for example) the higher centers are fairly low in energy while the reptile brain is charging ahead. The smarter parts of our brain just follow the lead of the primitive part.

In the nervous system, messages can only flow one way. The nerves that tell your muscle to turn the page of this booklet are called *afferent* nerves. They control things. They carry a message *to* the muscle. The nerves that tell you what the hand and arm are doing are completely separate. They are called *efferent* nerves, and they only carry messages back to the brain.

The interesting thing about the brain is that there are a lot more afferent pathways from the reptile brain up to the cortex than the other way around. When things get tough, Mother Nature has certainly designed the Reptile in us to be the boss! That is why it is so easy for us to do foolish things when we are angry. Our big brilliant brain full of insight and understanding is now working under the control of the reptile brain. Without some training on our part, that reptile brain will continue to control your brain when under stress.

This is Your Lizard Brain on Stress

There are three basic "stress responses" associated with the reptile brain. If the brain feels threatened, the reptile part takes over to assure survival. It does stuff that probably worked very well many thousands of years ago. The three choices are:

Fight: kill and eat the adversary.

Flight: run away.

Freeze: play dead.

The reptile brain is probably 90% to 100% selfish, so when people are being controlled by that part of their brain, you cannot expect much cooperation out of them. The best thing you can do is just wait for things to pass for the mood to change. Moods always change. There is really no point in discussing things while you or your partner are in bad moods. It is better to wait until the mood lightens up and things look brighter to you.

The reptile brain does not seem to be particularly emotional. It is more oriented toward action. To get to the emotion, we have to take a step up along the evolutionary ladder.

The Mammal Brain

Above the reptile brain we have a "paleomammalian brain." This part of our brain is what we see in primitive mammals. It is the part of the brain that it shows up in the higher animals. The higher animals have the ability to learn more and also the ability to cooperate and show unselfish behavior.

While all mammals have a reptile brain and while the reptile brain can still control the behavior of mammals, they also have a higher brain, and when they are using that, they cooperate well. Deer group together in herds to help each other be safe from predators. The wolves group together to help each other catch the deer. The mammals take much better care of their young than do reptiles. The mammal brain is perhaps 50% or more *cooperative* and is capable of acts of self-sacrifice, like the famous cat that went into a burning house several times, burning herself in the process, in order to rescue her own kittens. A reptile would have let them burn and maybe eaten their remains!

The Emotion-Generating Brain

This part of the brain is emotional. The limbic system and the cingulate gyrus light up like Christmas trees when a creature is experiencing strong emotions. Some times people tell me that they are too emotional, and that they wish they could be like Spock in Star Trek, completely logical and without emotions.

But that is not a worthy goal. The emotions have a valuable part to play. People who have suffered types of brain damage that removes their emotional brain from the equation have a strange deficit. They can't decide! The middle part of the brain is vital for helping us to make decisions. Without emotions, we are simply unable to decide what course of action we should pursue. So a person with damage to the emotional centers can calmly discuss whether to go to dinner or a movie and list the pros and cons of each path but they cannot decide.

Obviously the opposite is true too. People with too much of a certain emotion, such as fear or depression, are also unable to make decisions. There is certainly a line that must be walked, and too much or too little emotion does paralyze us. They key seems to be to be aware of our feelings, but not let them control us, or what we now call "emotional intelligence." We must acknowledge the emotion but not let it control us.

The Human Brain

Above the limbic system sits our Neocortex. This is the highest level of our brain. This neocortex actually forms about 5/6ths of our total brain tissue, and of that, the frontal cortex, the large lobes in the front of the brain, are the most impressive. The Prefrontal Lobes are the part of the cerebral cortex that makes us fully human. While our brains are much larger than other animals, our prefrontal lobes are where the real action is. We have large, powerful, creative, sensitive prefrontal lobes, and we are capable of greater acts of love, creativity, unselfishness, and cooperation than the rest of the creatures on this earth.

When we are at our best, we are like angels, intelligent and kind. So you can see why biologists like to say, we all have a lizard, a monkey, and an angel living inside of our head.

The Vital Switch

So what determines which part of our brain is in charge? Our brains also have little switches deep inside in them, the amygdalas. Our amygdalas are located on each side of our brains, midway between the corner of the eye and the ear. If you put your fingers over that spot, you have located your amygdala. They are about the size of a small almond. They sit underneath the cortex (the temporal lobes) and are hooked up to the hypocampus, our memory center.

The amygdala operates as a resource-shifter. When the front part of the amygdala is energized then your frontal lobe is energized. And when the back part of the amygdala is energized, then your reptile brain is getting all the energy!

Why "Will Power" Fails

Perhaps you have had trouble with your temper and you have made a promise to not do that again. You may have the right intention, but there is a problem. The location of the amygdala means that it is aware of the events around us before our conscious mind is. It is about a quarter of a second ahead of the conscious mind. It reacts to incidents before the consciousness becomes aware of them, That is why your passionate oath that you will never get angry like that again is doomed to fail. The part of the brain making the oath is not the part in charge of anger. It is as if you were to promise that *I* would pay all your future house payments. You cannot speak for me! You don't have the authority to do that! So please don't ever make a promise to never get angry again.

The reason for that lies in the question of timing. As you now know, the amygdala is ahead of your frontal lobes. So the shift of energy away from the frontal lobes and toward the alligator brain has happened before your consciousness is aware. It is very true that you can learn to control that reaction once it has happened. But the anger is already present before you can consciously control it.

I don't mean to suggest that you are not responsible for what happens when you are angry. You are responsible. But what we do know for sure is that anger happens ahead of the part of you we call the conscious mind. You are more than your conscious mind, and you are responsible for everything you do, not just what you do with full intent and careful planning.

So bear it mind that this book is not intended to blame you, but to give you choices you don't have. I am sure that through reading this book and doing the exercises, you will develop flexibility and choice in your responses.

Taming the Wild Amygdala

So, there is hope! In brain functioning there is a process we call *kindling*. This is the process of developing habits or patterns. If your amygdala is often switched forward, then it becomes easier and easier for you to be in a positive,

A client once told me jokingly that she seldom used her highest brain because she was anxious and depressed so much. She thought that when she died they could exhibit her brain as "hardly used, never been out of the box!"

There is truth to what she says. When our moods are always the same those moods become over-learned and habitual. It is as if our moods form "grooves" in the brain, so the mind always runs in the same groove. People get used to feeling and performing at certain levels, and to grow, you have to practice thinking outside of the grooves.

happy, and creative mood. In this state you are 100% cooperative and unselfish. Your own needs don't even come into the picture. You have forgotten yourself and are working for higher needs.

And the opposite is also true. When we stay in moods of depression, anxiety, anger, jealousy, and so on, the brain pathways become worn in, fixed if you will. The brain is ready and able to go to those unpleasant states of mind at the smallest provocation. So we can see that emotions are habit states, and by nurturing certain emotions we train our brain to experience those more and more easily. Like the physical body responding to physical exercise, practicing the positive means you have more positive.

Back in my graduate school days, we were taught that the brain doesn't grow and change. Now we know that is not true. The brain constantly grows, and like a muscle, when we exercise in certain ways, that part of the body - or the brain - grows. If you are angry, the anger "muscles" in your brain get stronger. If you exercise the opposite of anger, the opposite circuits get stronger.

Reflect on the usefulness of anger

Recognize that while anger is a natural part of ourselves, it is also generally not helpful. If you wish to live a more calm, intelligent, and effective life, start here. Think thoughtfully and deeply about how effective anger is in your life. How is it working so far?

You can see from reflecting on it that when we use anger we generally get no where. We might yell and storm at family members and they temporarily change. But soon they go right back to doing what they did before. So we yell and storm some more, which temporarily helps. But when you look at the whole picture, you see that being chronically angry does nothing to help create better situations. It just drives the problems under ground. And they do pop up again, don't they?

If you look at this problem pretty clearly and calmly, you can see that anger in families always creates backlash. Sooner or later, if you use anger it will come back to haunt you.

But I Apologized . . .

I have often seen a client asking for forgiveness for moments of anger, saying, "But what about all the good I do. Doesn't that make up for my anger?"

Actually, it doesn't seem to. The experience of anger is so powerful, so threatening, that people really never can forgive you, at least without a lot of hard work on their part. Good things that you may have done doesn't make up for it. Money, privileges, and even apologies don't seem to do the trick. Anger is just too strong and too unforgettable.

Perhaps you resent the fact that people don't seem to forgive you for your angry outbursts. That is understandable, but let's speak frankly. It does you no good to be angry about that. It is just how things are, and your anger about people not forgiving you won't change human nature. Anger is simply too traumatic. It alienates people, and they stay alienated for a very long time. The price you pay in the loss of love is much more than you can imagine.

Road rage

Perhaps you are close to agreement. "OK," you might say, "anger at family, or anger at co-workers, is not a smart strategy. What about anger with people outside of the family, such as those who drive in irresponsible ways? Aren't you justified in becoming angry with those people? After all, aren't they a menace to safe driving?"

Actually if you take a broad view, you will see that challenging a dangerous driver is just creating more danger. As we said, people are less intelligent when angry. They do irrational things. They act impulsively. Do you really want the bad driver in the other car acting even more irrationally and impulsively? Well, that is what you get when you try to correct their behavior. They get angry and therefore they are dumb and don't learn from what you are doing.

So getting angry with people in traffic is actually a problem of excessive optimism on your part. You really believe it will help them to be mad at them, but when you take a broader view, you can see that the anger didn't work. If you can rise above the question of whether you are justified in anger, and ask how it works, you will be on to something with real leverage.

What is the real result of anger?

Our challenge is to look at whether anger really helps. The comic Richard Pryor once set himself on fire while using drugs. He later said, "I jumped up, and I was on fire! And I ran out of the house on fire! And I ran down the street on fire! And I learned something from that. I learned that when you are on fire, running down the street, people get out of your way!"

Could looking at anger like that help you? Could you see an advantage to thinking that all anger does is to get people to jump back away from you, but it doesn't really help? It doesn't really change anything for the better? People you don't know generally learn nothing of value from your anger. People you are close to simply learn that they need to be fearful of you. Since fear and love cannot happen at the same time, anger is robbing you of the love that we all want and need.

Anger makes us feel "right." We are convinced we are more powerful and justified when we are angry. I know it is a pretty intoxicating feeling. But can I invite you to ask: "Would I rather be right or loved?"

A New View of Anger

Why not look at anger as a bad habit that grabbed onto you and has been interfering with your happiness and satisfaction ever since?

Suppose you think about habits generally. Don't we all have some good ones and some bad ones? If you simply see anger as a habit that is inefficient, you may feel some freedom from it. There is no value in blaming yourself or being angry at yourself because you have too much anger at others. If you are to develop some freedom from anger, start with yourself.

Many times, just looking at something in a new way is healthy. Please try out this idea about anger, that it really doesn't help. Try thinking of it as simply a habit. And see if you feel more free and healthy from that idea.

Now, you have begun to read my little book. Thank you. I enjoyed writing it; I hope you enjoy reading it. Can I invite you now to take one more step? Take a notebook and pen and jot down some of your thoughts about what you have read.

After all, if we could talk face to face, you could ask questions, challenge me, and learn more by the give-and-take of a heart to heart conversation. Why not give yourself an experience of having that conversation with yourself. Write down what you think about this chapter and what questions and objections come to mind. Try it. Pick up a pen and write a few thoughts.

Perhaps you are saying, "My problem is not that I am angry, but that I have to deal constantly with an angry person. What am I supposed to do about that?"

That certainly is a difficult problem. Angry people are hard to live with, work with . . . they are just plain difficult! I would never minimize that. In fact, some angry people can be truly dangerous. They can hurt or kill. Of course you suffer from living with or working for such a person.

As you read this book, you may want to see if your own view of anger changes. Perhaps you will come to learn how the brain switching works, and that will help you see patterns not just in the behavior of others, but also in the behavior of yourself.

Fear and escape are normal responses to anger. You may want to get away. That is understandable. It might even be the smartest thing to do. Some people really are dangerous, and their reptile brain will eventually cause them to kill someone. So the fear and flee response makes good sense.

Yet another response is anger in return. It is a tremendously "catching" emotion, one that spreads like wildfire. One angry person can soon create a whole group of angry people. Hitler, for example, led an entire nation into being controlled by anger. I have seen it over and over. In a therapy session with the whole family, one person gets angry and then others quickly follow.

So as I talk about how the amygdala works to shift energy away from the thought centers and down into the instinctive parts of the brain, perhaps it will benefit you to recognize that your own brain works just the same. Flight, fight, freeze . . . they all come from the reptile brain. They are all part of an unthinking reaction.

This book is intended to promote deep thinking, and some good reflection on anger. At the end of most chapters there is a section in italics. That italicized section is designed to speak directly to you, a person who is coping with someone who uses anger. That section will speak to your interests, and suggest some skills for you to develop. The main portion of this book is designed to help that person who has allowed anger to influence him (or her) too much. With these chapter end-notes, I hope it helps you, too.

Now, can I respectfully ask you to begin to keep a diary? Can you take a minute to write down some of your own thoughts about this chapter? Would you let me invite you to begin your own journey of growth and discovery?

Chapter Two

What Causes Anger?

"He who angers you conquers you."
– Elizabeth Kenny

He really made me mad! The most common way we have of understanding anger is that it is a reaction to what happens to us. As we watch people deal with emotions, it does seem likely that events and people do make us mad. After all, something happens and then there is an angry response.

Let's be fair. People sometimes say we are responsible for all of our feelings, but that goes too far. There is some truth to the understanding that people make us mad. After all, you are likely to become angry with someone on the road who honks aggressively or who flashes rude hand gestures. In our own families, we are more likely to be angry when others contradict or argue or discount us. Our amygdalas are constructed in such a way as to make it almost impossible to not react to a threat. But that is just a surface analysis. Let's look deeper.

How Our Thinking Controls Us

Actually, there is a combination of what happens to us and what kinds of thoughts we typically entertain in our minds that causes anger. You can do a quick mental experiment to prove that this is true.

Imagine five men, all the same age, all with the same general background. In each case, a rude driver cuts each man off, honks aggressively, and makes the exact same rude gesture. Does each man become equally angry? Of course not. It is immediately obvious that each man will react differently. One is furious, one is annoyed, one is amused by the immaturity shown, one feels guilty, and one didn't even notice. What accounts for the difference? It lies in the *habits of thinking* of each person.

Variety of Thinking Habits

One man has a habit of thinking more peacefully, and he thinks that people who are rude in traffic are silly and short-sighted. This man has cultivated compassion. So he feels sorry for someone so silly as to act that way.

Another man is in the habit of thinking that the world is full or rotten, no-good people and they need to be put in their place. Does it surprise you to see that the second man becomes quite angry?

A Better View

As you see, I encourage you to view the problem of anger as based on our own habits, not something that others cause us to feel. Outside events can only work with our own habits of thinking. That is a better view because it means there is something that we can do about anger.

If anger were caused by other people, there would be no hope. You would go through your life reacting as you always have, and you could never change. My view is that we are ultimately responsible for how we feel. I do not think you can immediately control how you feel, but you can take a long view, analyze your patterns and habits, and eventually make a difference.

Sometimes people resist this view because they are secretly fearful of "being to blame" for the anger. That is understandable. Many people grow up in families where "who is to blame" is an important question. The theory seems to be that if we can find out who is to blame and punish him, everything will be better.

This childhood fear is really groundless. When we take responsibility for our own feelings, we actually begin to feel more free and flexible. We are no longer slaves of what other people do to us. The world has more possibilities.

Is Anger Ever Positive?

We do sometimes see people who have suppressed anger, who have kept it inside and never spoken up about what they want. They were never peaceful and insightful, and they were also never obviously angry. Instead they kept it bottled up inside. They tell us that getting "in touch with anger" was a helpful experience for them. It gave them the energy to get up and do what needed to be done. So there are times when anger produces a good outcome. For those people, acknowledging anger is an important positive step. It isn't the end of the journey, just a first step.

So if you happen to be a person with anger "bottled up" inside, you may be doing yourself some real damage. This book may help you find a way to deal with that anger. Some therapists recommend you yell into a towel or beat a throw rug. That sometimes helps. Your anger needs to be understood and dealt with. There is no problem with you getting in touch with it, in these limited cases.

The problem is that *most often*, people misuse anger. Folks who are already able to express it, are misusing it. The use of anger to get our way is not helpful. It makes other people angry, so we end up with a world full of angry people. When we get our way because of our anger, we haven't really earned the changes. Other people are not cooperating with us, and they are clearly not changing what they do out of enlightened self interest or from love and respect for us. Instead, they do it because they are afraid of our anger.

So anger is a way to have an impact, but it is cheating, a form of emotional blackmail. Instead of earning respect and mutual cooperation, we are forcing others to bend to our will. That will always have a high price.

If you are bottling up anger, I suggest you write some very sincere, honest letters, deeply heartfelt. Express to people in your life how you really feel. Tell them the things that you have been bottling up.

Now, rather than send those letters, find a sympathetic friend. Read her or him those letters, *and then burn them!*

Repeat this process several times, until you begin to recognize when you are angry. You are more aware of your own inner processes. This will help. But I would discourage you from using that anger to make the other person see your point of view.

Later in the book, you will learn some ways of speaking to people about what you want. These ways of talking, what I call speaking from your heart, are much more helpful than expressing your anger to someone. So the write-read-burn cycle is only to help heal you of suppressed anger.

If you want to live calmly and thoughtfully, you must live

openly and honestly. You must learn to speak from your heart, and that means you have to know what is in your heart. Sincerely standing up and saying what you really believe and know is the foundation for peace.

An Overlooked Anger Trigger

If you use alcohol or drugs, you might find your anger is worse. As we have been discussing the role of the lower levels of brain activity, you may have already realized that any drugs or alcohol use will reduce the effectiveness of your brain.

Remember that the highest level of the brain, the cortex, is responsible for our highest and best behavior. When we use alcohol, the cortex is the first thing to be affected. Obviously, if you start to have some kind of conflict and you have been drinking, the results are not going to be pretty.

How do you know if drugs or alcohol play a part?

- Do people ever talk to you about your alcohol or drug use?

- Do you ever need a drink to "get going" in the mornings?

- Have you ever had a blackout or clouded memory after drug or alcohol use?

- Do you find you use alcohol / drugs every day?

- When you examine your own angry responses, can you see a pattern of using drugs or alcohol associated with them?

Certainly if there is some kind of substance abuse problem going on you are not going to be successful at transforming your anger into peace or cooperation. You just don't have the brain power.

On the other hand, you might try an experiment. Just see how you do if you discontinue using drugs or alcohol. Just experiment. I recall a patient who told me about his high school use of marijuana. He would go to his room, open his window and smoke a joint. Then he would study. He thought that smoking marijuana would help him relax so he could study better. I had to explain to him that there is a phenomenon called *state dependent learning*. What that means is that if we put a substance into our brain and then learn something, we cannot recall what we have learned unless the same substance is in our brain when we are trying to recall it.

He grinned ruefully and said, "Well, that would explain why I was failing all my classes, wouldn't it?"

He finally quit marijuana and found that his life was better. It is a fact that there is no substance you can take that makes your brain function better in all ways. Everything we have looked at does impair the brain in some way. If you are using, you probably ought to consider quitting, just to see how it works for you.

This may not be easy to do. Sometimes the habit of substance abuse is so strong that it makes it almost impossible for you to quit on your own.

If that is the case, consider AA and other self help groups. If you find you are suffering serious withdrawal symptoms, you may even need some medical help. This is called "detoxification" or detox, and it can be a life saver. Don't hesitate to reach our for some help if you find you are feeling nausea, sweating, shakiness, and other signs of withdrawal.

There are many ways out of the substance abuse habit. Some people successfully quit all on their own. Others use AA and other groups. Many find help through psychotherapy. All of these do work.

What will not work is just continuing to do what you have always done, continuing to use.

Fear of Giving Up Anger

Sometimes we are actually afraid to give up something even when it doesn't work. We don't know what we will replace it with. That is a reasonable fear. You should be cautious about giving up something that you know. I support you being cautious. All I will try to do in this book is give you some useful information.

Through this book we will be examining ways to make your life work well without anger. I would encourage you to take a rather broad view at this point. After all, retraining our amygdala is hard work, and you wouldn't want to jump into such a challenging task without thinking it through rather carefully.

A Broader View

Reflecting on the problem you will see that some people do not get angry and their lives work well. Perhaps you can develop some curiosity about how they do that, and how you could learn more of how to do that? Oh, you might be thinking that everyone gets just as angry as you do, but a bit of logic will expose the flaw in that argument. Not everyone is as tall, as smart, or as talented. People vary on all kinds of attributes. So it is reasonable to suppose that your level of anger is unique to you, and that other people may not experience the same level.

Thinking on times when something was better can be very

enlightening. Perhaps you have experienced times in your own life when you felt calm and peaceful, when nothing bad was going on, and you were effective and had positive impact. Recalling that time might be rather pleasant for you. Wouldn't it be great to be able to live that way all the time?

What was behind your best times? When you were the most calm and peaceful, what seems to have been the cause of that? Was there something you were doing to help that happen? Would you like more of that?

Homework Experiment

Writing things down is a wonderful way to make changes. Keep a diary about your anger; write down when you feel angry and what happened. The very act of documenting what you are doing will energize your frontal lobes and bring energy back to the smartest part of you.

If you will simply begin to write things down, this book will have much more value to you. Reading is passive; writing is active. Activity helps us learn; passivity doesn't. Otherwise, we could learn to play the cello by watching Yo Yo Ma on television. I have tried it, and I still can't play.

Oh, you can read this short book in not much time. But you will not get much value from that. Only if you actually work at the book will it be of help to you. The famous psychiatrist, David Burns (author of *Feeling Good: The New Mood Therapy* as well as many other fine books), likes to tell his patients that in spite of being a well-known author, he is actually only a very average therapist. He then explains: That means that if his patients get better, they have to do a lot of work!

He then will playfully say that he had a list of psychiatrists in the Philadelphia area who didn't require their patients work hard. He offered to let the patient see that list. Throughout the years, Burns said, people would chuckle and say they got the point. One fellow, though, said, "Well, I would like to see that list!"

So what do you say? Would you try the simple experiment? Or do you want a book that doesn't ask you to work? Getting the most from this book takes work on your part. Get a notebook and begin to document your thoughts and reactions. Write down what you have read that strikes you, either as sensible or silly. Write your own thoughts, you emotional reactions. Write what you want, and how you want to achieve it. And especially begin to write about the events that make you angry.

Write!

Do you tend to blame yourself for the anger of others? If you are in a relationship where you love someone who tends to be too angry, then perhaps you do.

But is that really fair? Maybe not! Perhaps you have been trying to keep the other person from getting angry. So when the anger comes, you rush around to try to make the angry person happy again. You imagine you have caused that anger.

It may not have occurred to you that by your fearfulness toward the angry individual, you are actually training him to be more angry. You are rewarding the anger.

Am I saying to refuse to cooperate? Not at all. I just want you to reflect on how you might be enabling the very thing you hate.

And I am not saying to fight with angry people, either. You have to find a way to keep your cool when the heat gets turned up. The point is, don't take it to heart. You didn't cause him to be mad, he did, and he will have to fix it himself.

If you are dealing with an angry person, you can do the same thing as I ask him or her to do. Keep your own diary. What do you want? What are you doing to achieve your goals? What frightens you? What motivates you?

Too often when we are around an angry person, we become angry or frightened ourselves, so our brains don't work either. In your diary, ask yourself, if the anger miraculously disappeared, what do you want in its place? Write about your goals and intentions. Write about your dreams.

This diary will become your field of play, where you try out new ideas and beliefs. It will be a place where you can be honest and sincere, where you can speak of what is hidden and explore what is forbidden.

It is where you can truly be yourself.

Write!

Chapter Three

What is Behind Anger?

Of the Seven Deadly Sins, anger is possibly the most fun. To lick your wounds, to smack your lips over grievances long past, to roll over your tongue the prospect of bitter confrontations still to come, to savor to the last toothsome morsel both the pain you are given and the pain you are giving back -- in many ways it is a feast fit for a king. The chief drawback is that what you are wolfing down is yourself. The skeleton at the feast is you.
 – Frederick Buechner

What is behind the anger we feel? There are two general answers to that: insecurity and the appetite to control others. Let's think together about them.

Insecurity

First, most often there is a feeling of *insecurity*. When we feel fearful, out of control, or threatened, we might respond with anger. Clearly the feeling of insecurity is not one we tolerate well. Insecurity seems to say to us, "I am NOT OK." What an unwelcome feeling! We don't seem to be able to admit we have such a feeling. Instead we flee to a feeling where we feel more in control, that of indignation or resentment or even rage. In all of those we feel more of a "I am OK, and you are not OK."

So you can see this type of anger – the most common kind – as a *defense*, something that allows us to manage uncomfortable emotions. Because it is a defense, when we use it, we aren't learning. The purpose of a defense is to keep things just as they are, to avoid change. It is like retreating behind a castle wall when the enemy is outside. Nothing gets in or out. We hunker down and try to ride out the problem. Anger keeps you from learning anything new.

Put Your Diary to Work

If you keep a diary of the things that make you angry, you may discover that is the case. Just before the anger, there may have been a moment of insecurity, and you fled that feeling and into anger. Just becoming aware of that allows us a more powerful option, namely one of vulnerability. Honesty. Openness.

That may seem ridiculous. After all, what is to be gained by focusing your attention on the insecure feeling instead of being angry? Anger doesn't want you to acknowledge the vulnerable feeling. Anger wants you to obey it, to keep the angry behavior. After all, anger says, how could it possibly help to expose your real feelings?

The Power of Honesty

The answer is that when we acknowledge our real feeling of insecurity, people tend to be more understanding and accepting. They might listen better. They may be able to have some empathy for us. This starts us on a path toward negotiating a reasonable agreement. It is much better than anger.

After all, you already know that when you show anger at people, their reaction is either anger coming right back at you, or fear. Both reactions reduce their intelligence. So your intelligence is reduced, theirs is reduced. And, as we read earlier, people do get out of your way. But both of you are less intelligent, and both of you suffer from rigid thinking and reduced creativity. No wonder you can never seem to solve a problem when angry!

But when you speak honestly and without anger, something else happens. The higher parts of the brain light up and the other person listens in a completely different way. Instead of trying to get your way, you are simply talking from your heart. And they listen from their heart.

I don't mean if you do that once, it will change everything. Honesty has power, but it may take months of effort for you to undo the damage you have done with your anger. What I do mean is that if you speak from your heart, and keep it up over a long time, you will notice a difference, a delightful difference in how people listen to you.

The Value of Anger

Most often we do find some kind of anxiety, fear, or insecurity behind the anger. There is a moment in which there is a flash of fear, and the anger come up as a way of managing that fear. In the wild, this reaction is helpful. If you are caught by a predator you feel a flash of fear, and then you begin to fight for your life. Occasionally that burst of anger helps you to escape. We are the children of those who fought and escaped.

Another example of how this anger helps is during courtship. If you are facing a rival for your loved one's affection, you feel fear, a fear of loss. That might be followed by some anger that you use to drive the rival away. Nature programs on public television are full of this kind of contest, where a bull elk drives away the younger suitors. Part of our heritage is that instinct to drive away rivals. In our primitive heritage, we brought down a kill, then had to use anger to drive away others who wanted to eat our food.

So even if we look angry and controlling, the chances are good that the angry actions are actually triggered by insecurity. In the primitive conditions where we are bashing rivals with a club or trying to fight for our share of the just-killed antelope, the insecurity-anger link works well. Of course, in modern society, there is little to be gained from that instinctive reaction. If your spouse were being courted by a rival, bashing someone's head only lands you in jail!

Perfectionism's False Promise

Perfectionism refers to people who feel strongly that things should be "perfect" or in other words, they way they want things to be. Perfectionism is a habit that comes in two flavors: self-focused and other-focused. The self-focused people are angry at themselves, they just aren't doing enough, being enough, and pleasing enough. Their anger at themselves is a type of depression. "How could I have been so stupid?" they ask. "What is wrong with me? Why didn't I do better?"

But something turned against the self can turn against others too. Criticizing others, pointing out their faults and flaws, showing others how they should have done something different are all forms of other-directed perfectionism. It is anger based on a kind of insecurity. The fear is that if things are not *just so* then it will be awful! Some authority figure (parents, neighbors, God) will be angry if things aren't perfect. The perfectionist's own anger is a disguised way of staying out of trouble themselves! If I get mad at you for not being perfect, their thinking runs, then *I* cannot possibly be blamed.

Blame is the key here. The insecurity is about that: blame for an inadequate performance. If you find yourself criticizing others a good deal, perhaps it would be enlightening to you to discover who you are really afraid of.

Perfectionism promises more than it can deliver. This habit claims that by trying to make things perfect, you will be happy. Research into perfectionism contradicts its claim. The opposite is true. The more perfectionistic one is, the more unhappiness. Happiness doesn't come from getting what we want, but in being grateful for what we have.

I must be honest here. Perfectionism is a very stubborn habit to change. It has a lot of tricks to let it stay in control of you. People who have been influenced by perfectionism, who have been controlled by it, are terribly unhappy, but there is a profound fear that without it they might be even more miserable! "Yes," Perfectionism says, "you are unhappy now, but just think of how awful things would be if you didn't constantly try to be perfect! Things would be awful. Life would be a catastrophe. Just keep criticizing, and soon the people around you will get it and shape up, and then you will be happy."

Please trust me on this. Perfectionism is lying to you. It will never deliver. You will continue all through your life, your time on earth will come to an end, and you will still be miserable and lonely. Perfectionism contributes to anxiety, depression, and anger. Life is a messy business, and we all make mistakes. Criticizing myself for a mistake just makes me less likely to try something new. Criticizing my employee or co-worker for a mistake makes them less likely to put their whole heart into a project. The anxiety that things will not be good enough seems like a convincing idea at the time. When we look at the bigger picture, we see how very counterproductive it really is.

Control

As I work with angry people, their spouses and co-workers accuse them of being control addicts. There is some truth to this, of course. There is insecurity, but it diminishes with the effort to control the situation. Such angry people can easily be helped. When this person acknowledges and deals with the underlying fears, we see great progress. Most of the time, this is the kind of control we see when someone uses anger to control.

There is another type of individual. Some people enjoy controlling others, not out of insecurity but paradoxically out of too much security. These folks feel entitled to dominate and control. They have self esteem

Joe was dragged into my office by his wife, who was tired of his yelling and intimidating her and their three children.

Joe's childhood was one where his father dominated and domineered and his mother meekly submitted, so he could see absolutely nothing wrong. He rejected my suggestions that one is less intelligent when one is angry. He felt more intelligent, more powerful. Why change?

I asked him to imagine that we are in a small airplane over the Rockies. It is dark, stormy, and one of the engines is having trouble. Would Joe want an angry pilot, or a calm pilot?

Immediately Joe replied, "I'd want an angry pilot. He'd pull us through for sure!"

The counseling eventually failed and Joe's wife left him. She couldn't respect or love a bully.

that is too high, not too low. Their self-esteem is unrealistic. They think they can do no wrong.

These people, the control addicts, can be very dangerous people. They take pleasure from anger, and from causing pain. When most of us get angry, our heart rate speeds up. When the pathological control individuals get angry, their heart rate slows down, and they get icy calm. They might do anything in order to boss and control. They often are brutal.

The analogy to the primitive society is that in any group there are bullies. Among predatory animals there are also bullies. Whether we study bears or people, we find criminal behavior. The bully who takes pleasure in causing pain is a criminal. We don't have good treatment for these people. They generally cannot be helped. No matter how much a counselor talks, no matter what the consequences, these people continue to feel completely entitled to control and dominate. Their type of anger is an icy, not a hot anger. There is no insecurity that a counselor can work with. The only solution is to get away from them. I hope you are not one of them.

Effects of Anger

Now let's talk about the advantages of shifting away from chronic anger.

Studies on emotional training found that just a few minutes of either anger or peace would influence the body for up to six hours later. Measuring a marker of immune function - the processes the body uses to fight off infection - they found that a few minutes of anger suppressed the immune system for six hours or more. That is just one simple episode of anger! During those six hours the anger subjects in this experiment were more vulnerable to infection and less able to heal.

On the other hand, comparison subjects who were experiencing a few minutes of peace showed the opposite effect. Their immune system was boosted to unusually high levels. They were experiencing greater health, and this effect too lasted for six hours. There is a simple reason for this. Peace is our body's favorite state, and it will reward you with better immune system and lower blood pressure.

Other research has shown that men who are often angry, who express anger to others, are more at risk for heart attacks than those who are typically calm. Anger raises blood pressure, lowers the immune functions, and makes us more prone to stress illnesses. Let's see why this is.

Living Better Through Chemistry

There is a master hormone in your body called *pregnenalone*. It can be converted by your body into other hormones. We are going to focus on one of two hormones, produced by the adrenal glands. These are produced depending on what your body needs. The two are *cortisol* and *DHEA*.

Cortisol is the stress hormone. When you need sudden energy, it will do the trick. But when you have high cortisol levels for long periods of time, you get lots of bad side effects. Blood pressure goes up. You put on fat. You feel exhausted. Your muscles begin to waste away. Your immune system suffers, causing you to get more infections. High levels of cortisol are seen in people who suffer from chronic depression, and it appears that as patients recover from depression, the cortisol level drops.

DHEA (dihydroepiandrosterone) is often called "the youth hormone." When you have plenty of DHEA, your blood pressure goes down. Your body uses up body fat, giving you more of a lean body. Your skin looks better, less wrinkled, and your immune system is stronger. As we get older, our DHEA begins to drop, but people who have good humor and a peaceful outlook on life keep the DHEA levels more like when they were young. If you can achieve an immunity to anger, if you can live in good spirits and with a peaceful outlook, you will live a longer and healthier life!

You should not take DHEA as a supplement unless it is prescribed by a doctor who will track your DHEA-S blood levels. It is much better to use natural methods to raise the DHEA level. Good spirits, good attitude, practicing gratitude and forgiveness, and meditation will raise the DHEA level in your blood without resorting to potentially dangerous supplements.

So consider the message of this book as one way to raise your DHEA level, and keep yourself younger.

Relationship Leverage

Pretend for a minute that anger was really a force that can control others. When Anger begins to control a person, it promises respect, love, and loyalty from those around. Anger says, "If you obey my rules and intimidate people, you will not have any more problems."

Don't believe Anger. It is lying to you.

Perhaps you have believed that lie. Now step back. In reality, the people around will only pretend to respect, love, and be loyal to you. In reality, the respect drops each time anger rises. Love flees, and loyalty leaves.

May I make an analogy? I have done a good deal of work with adolescents using marijuana, and often at the beginning of therapy they really like that drug. They believe it makes them smarter and more capable. They genuinely believe they perform better when they are using marijuana than when they are not. Then I have to begin to tell them the painful truth. What marijuana does, is to make us pleased with mediocre performance. It makes us happy with doing less than our best. All the research shows that performance declines but satisfaction increases.

They are happier but more stupid.

Anger is like that. It promises more than it delivers. Like a drug, it makes you feel strong and invulnerable, and each moment you are getting closer to being abandoned and rejected.

The Key is in Your Hand

The key is in developing habits of happiness, appreciation, and peacefulness. Under these conditions, the pregnenolone gets transformed into DHEA. We feel better, our body starts to heal, we have a better immune system . . . lots of good things are happening. It may seem ironic to you – it does to me – that when we choose a path of peace and appreciation, the very hormones in our body make that pathway easier. And if we choose a path of anger and resentment, the cortisol itself makes us more angry. Whatever path we choose will turn out to be supported by our own body!

Try an Experiment

In your diary, begin to note when you feel physically the best. Keep track of that for a week. I predict you will learn that physical wellness and emotional peacefulness go hand in hand. But please don't take my word for it. Track it yourself! Jot down how well or unwell you felt during the day. Rate it from 1 - 10, with 10 = on top of the world, and 1 = horrible. When you feel worse, see if you can track back and see what you were feeling, like anger or fear. See if you can link your physical health to emotions.

If you struggle to help a loved one overcome anger, sometimes you can talk about your own goals of wanting to respect and love them, but at the same time feeling that love slip away when the anger comes up. Point out that well known saying in the Bible, "A perfect love drives out fear." By the same token, high fear drives out love.

You can admit to being human: If you were perfect, you could have love for a person who is often angry at you. But you are not perfect. You are only human. You cannot love with perfect love. As a human being, you can only love with the limited human love with which we are capable.

Maybe your partner isn't ready to hear that. Maybe you will just hear more anger coming back at you. If so, that means the time is not right.

But you can do something. You can write in your

diary about your goals. You can talk to yourself about the honest truth that being on the receiving end of anger does drive out the love.

Sometimes people will cry, "I just want to be loved unconditionally!" We hear of this 'unconditional love' and it sounds wonderful. I have to break some bad news to you: There isn't any on this planet.

At least, among humans there isn't any. I am convinced that dogs are more capable of unconditional love than humans, and as such, perhaps they are God's gift to the human race, to remind us of something we can strive for but never attain. But on this planet, there is no person capable of unconditional love. Don't pretend for a moment to be one. Don't even agree that you should try. Embrace your human limitations. You are not capable of loving someone that you fear.

Just as love and fear cannot coexist, so also intimidation drives out respect and loyalty. We run from predators. We don't love them. Respect? Well, yes, but from a distance, and the more distance, the better.

What does your loved one want? Ask if love or fear is the goal.

We can't have it both ways.

Chapter Four

Immunity to Anger

No problem can ever be solved by the consciousness that created it. We must learn to see the world anew.
– Albert Einstein

Note: This chapter can be read in a few minutes, but it contains steps that should take several days or even a week or two to accomplish. If you go through these exercises carefully, you will harvest rich results.

What if Anger were a kind of disease, like an infection that you might get from being around someone who is already infected? What if we looked at anger and something that no one *wanted* to experience, but a feeling that we are all vulnerable to? Could we reduce our vulnerability?

When we are young, we get vaccinations and inoculation against a variety of illnesses. Then we don't have to fear polio or typhoid. Our bodies are immune. Can we do the same thing with anger?

Yes we can. And when we become less susceptible to anger, we are free to develop better ways of dealing with problems and difficulties. There is a simple three-step process that will give you your own immunity to anger. First you must set a goal. Second, you must desensitize yourself to the anger triggers. And third, you have to teach your brain to see the world in a new way.

If you have come this far with me, I think we agree on a goal.

Next, we will work on desensitization. It is like allergy shots. A child who receives desensitization shots to an allergy is able to feel comfortable and free to do things that he couldn't do before. Like that child, you will increase your comfort and freedom when outside forces cannot disturb your own peace of mind.

What is the Opposite?

When I talk to clients trying to overcome anger, their goal is usually to not be angry. There is a problem with that type of a goal. It is negative, an absence of something. I have learned that positive goals, where we are moving *toward* something, are motivational. They call to us. But just to 'get away' from something is not. So ask yourself, when you find you are trying to get rid of a habit, what is the opposite?

Most people say the opposite is when they feel a peaceful and calm feeling. Everyone has moments when he or she feels that. You have felt those feelings. Perhaps not often, perhaps not every day, but you have. Those positive feelings can become a road map out of Anger Land.

Use Your Diary

I suggest you add awareness of positive emotional states to your diary. Notice when you are most peaceful and calm. Jot down the circumstances, and expand on that in your diary.

Noticing spontaneous good feelings has a powerful effect. You will notice more of them. What we notice, we tend to repeat. Without even consciously trying, you are developing an ability to be calm and peaceful. I am certain that if you write each day, with just a little reflection you will recall a time during the day that you felt quite positive. Write specifically about things that have happened in your life today that you would like to have continue.

This practice is called "the gratitude diary." We now know that writing down three to five things each day that we feel good about has a remarkable effect on our moods. In one recent study, keeping a gratitude diary was more effective in treating depression than any other single treatment, including medication. If you start to keep a gratitude diary, it will help you replace the feeling of anger with positive feelings. Try it!

Practice Feeling Good

If you wanted to learn to play a musical instrument, there is no other way to do it than to practice. Your emotions are like music, they can be harmonious or they can be strident and clashing.

Take the next step. If you have been tracking good feelings, and noticing more and more of them, you can now bring those feelings to mind as an exercise. If you will practice ten minutes of quiet and calm feeling every day, this will greatly help you recognize times during the day that you are spontaneously calm. There are instructions in the **appendix** on some simple and effective ways to practice calmness. Read the pages on Controlled Breathing and on Autogenic Training. People who practice disciplines like those do have less reactive amygdalas. DHEA rises and the body is more healthy. The immune system is stimulated and you are resistant to illnesses.

If you will practice autogenic training once or twice a day, for ten to twenty minutes each time, stresses will not bother you as much; you will be more resilient and shrug off troubles easier. You will also fall asleep faster and sleep more soundly. Research into sleep problems shows that regular meditation does help.

This is actually quite important. You really do have to practice some kind of relaxation skill at this point. Just reading passively will not help.

If you were in my office and we were working on freeing you from anger, I would give you the Autogenic Training as an assignment and ask you to practice it every day. Practice at least once a day. Twice a day is excellent, and I have had some patients practice five times a day, and of course, they progressed much more rapidly. One woman practiced before leaving for work, at her mid-morning break, after lunch, during the afternoon break, and when she got home from work. She suffered from irritable bowel syndrome and was able to completely stop the painful spasms with that regimen.

Desensitize Yourself to "Triggers"

Desensitization means to make ourselves less sensitive to something. If you were allergic to certain things like pollens in the air, your doctor might prescribe desensitization shots for you. You would be given very diluted versions of the allergen. Slowly you would become less sensitive to it, and you would soon be free of your hay fever or allergies.

Actually allergies are not caused by outside substances, they are caused by our body's reaction to them. If you are allergic to peanut butter, you might die if you ate it, but I am not and I can eat it freely. So it is not the peanut butter itself that kills allergic people, it is their own reactions to that. So it is with anger. The events don't make you angry, the anger is the result of your own inner thinking habits.

What are the triggers?

You can probably think of certain events that trigger your anger. Perhaps it is someone driving in a stupid and reckless fashion, or someone following you too closely. Or maybe it is events in the family.

Write down each thing that you can think of that irritates or enrages you. Estimate how much each item on your list bothers you. Put a number by each item, where 1 = no bother at all, and 10 = the most maddening thing I can think of. Be sure to write down the *very first sign* that something is about to make you angry. These are your triggers, your allergens if you will.

This is very important. You must write down the triggers. Sometimes you may feel embarrassed. You may think, "These are silly, they aren't that big a deal."

Write them anyway. This is not a time for embarrassment. It is a time for courage and honesty.

Desensitization

Now when you practice quieting yourself, also begin to practice picturing the events on the list. Each time you think of the upsetting situation, breath deeply and slowly and concentrate on relaxing your muscles. Keep that up until you have a relaxed and calm reaction even while picturing the upsetting situation. Even though the same event happens ('My spouse yells angrily at me'), you will find now that it just doesn't have the power to disturb you! You have tamed the wild amygdala. You have achieved control over that situation! It can no longer control you, and you are more free.

Use your rating system. After each practice, rate how much the issue now bothers you. Hopefully you will find that it starts to feel less and less upsetting. Your rating begins to come down.

You may have to expose yourself to each trigger dozens of times in order to desensitize yourself. That is only reasonable and right. Our brains have very few afferent nerves from the higher centers to the lower. The amygdalas are slow to get over fears. It takes considerable time and effort to control anger. After all, fifty thousand years ago, most of our problems could be solved by bashing them with clubs (or running or playing dead!) but today that is not true. Our brains are not really designed to live in civilized society without some training.

See The World Anew

Now that you have controlled the trigger, look deeper. When something triggers your anger, you have an assumption about the *meaning* of that behavior. If a rude driver upsets you, what do you believe about that driver? That he deserves to be taught a lesson? If a family member upsets you, what do you believe about that? Perhaps that she is not showing respect? *Write down the beliefs you have when you find anger is controlling you.*

What could another explanation be? Try to take a broader view. Look for a more peaceful way to view the situation.

Maybe the person in traffic has to rush because he just heard of an emergency? Maybe your family member is not thinking clearly or is distracted?

Look at the situation again. Practice compassion and understanding. Wouldn't your body do better if this didn't mean a catastrophe? Can you see a more soothing way to look at it?

- Could there be a <u>positive intention</u> even if the behavior is bad?
  "He's just trying to be playful and friendly." or, "She is trying to reduce her own discomfort."

- Could there be a <u>hidden benefit</u> that comes from the situation?
  "This is an opportunity for me to learn patience."

- Are their <u>compensating factors</u>?
  "She is generally much more positive, she must just be in a bad mood."
  "He is a great boss to work for because of the challenges, and I can overlook his temper tantrums."

- Will it <u>soon pass</u> and is therefore not an important issue?
  "Our finances are generally bad at this time of year, but in three months we will be fine."

If you discover a better way to view the trigger, a way that allows you to feel more compassion about the person who makes you angry, then you will be immune to anger - well, at least less controlled by it - in that situation. You have increased your freedom. Keep focusing on finding a broader view, and soon you will find that you feel generally more peaceful and relaxed. You will find your thinking is clearer and people around you will feel more relaxed and at ease.

Now you see things anew. You have more freedom to use your whole brain, and you will be more creative and innovative.

EXERCISE

Keep a small notebook you can carry with you. When you get an angry feeling coming on you, quickly jot down the thoughts you have. You can desensitize yourself to that trigger and it will free you up tremendously. By finding a broader way to see the situation, you will become desensitized to it. Follow these steps:

1. What is going on? Describe it in behavioral terms.

2. What do you think that means? Explore this thoroughly. Try to figure out what your underlying beliefs are that make you vulnerable to anger. Detail those beliefs.

3. How does it feel to you when you believe those things? Do you enjoy that feeling, or is it hard on you?

4. What is another way to look at this situation? How would you feel if you genuinely believed that way of seeing it?

5. Fill in this sentence: "This is actually *good*, because . . ." If you look for a way to see it with acceptance or even appreciation, you will find it.

What if it isn't working?

Some people have a very difficult time with this homework. No matter how hard they try, they seem to continue to be provoked and irritated by the triggers. If you are in this situation, perhaps you should consider another possibility. Your anger may be a symptom of depression. Not all depressed people are angry, and not all angry people are depressed. Most often the two are not related. But sometimes they are.

You might want to take a simple checklist of depression symptoms to see how you score. If you find that you are depressed, consider treatment. In the appendix, there is a depression checklist. If you score more than 17 on this checklist, you are clearly in the depressed range, and do need some treatment.

What kind of treatment? Frankly, all treatments for depression are the same. Psychotherapy helps a great deal; medication helps a great deal. Combining the two seems to add a benefit. If you do choose medication, you definitely should add some counseling. If you want to simply do counseling without medication, that will work out fine.

Psychotherapy is a good bet if you know a talented therapist. The particular type of therapy - that means, cognitive therapy, or interpersonal therapy, or insight therapy - doesn't matter in the least. All therapies work equally well. The real difference is in the therapist, not in the therapy. The best research shows clearly that some therapists are 'supershrinks,' most are "shrinks" and some are what we would call 'pseudoshrinks.' While the 'supershrinks' seem to help about anyone they see, the 'pseudoshrinks' do very little good, and actually can do harm. So if you don't seem to hit it off with a counselor, try someone else. It probably isn't your fault.

Medications are also about the same, but here there is a difference depending on your own body chemistry. The old standbys, such as Prozac ® work as well as the newer ones. But some people don't respond well to some medications, and at times several changes must be made. New dual action antidepressants (working on both the seratonin and norepinepherine systems) seem to be slightly better than the older seratonin focused drugs.

A fairly new development is with omega-3 oils and depression. There are several good studies that show a strong positive effect on people with stubborn depression. It seems that the omega-3 oils (such as those found in fish) have a very good impact on depression. Taking 1 - 4 grams a day seems to be a good dose. Four grams may be slightly better than 1 gram. You aren't going to overdose.

Look into "grass-fed beef" as a source of omega-3 oils. A bit of research on the internet will tell you a good deal about why we should not feed our cattle grains.

If you are a vegetarian, flax oil will convert into omega-3 oil in the body; take a couple of tablespoons a day. Flax seeds won't digest unless you grind them up. I put them on my cereal in the morning. I don't like the taste, but they are good for me. Put two or three tablespoons in a coffee grinder, so break them up. Eating walnuts is a somewhat good source of omega-3 precursors. Use canola oil to cook with. Eat lots more dark green vegetables.

What about if you are dealing with angry people? Well, the same homework does apply to you.

It is understandable that you attribute your negative feelings to the angry person. But that doesn't really give you the leverage you need to cope. You will need to decide that working on your own inner reactions is really the key. You have to look at how you can be more powerful and have more positive influence if you practice calmness and peace.

Desensitization is vital. You also have to train your own brain to react with thoughtfulness and calm when someone is 'pressing your buttons' so to speak. You also have to practice some meditation every day, so that your own health is good and your brain is used to being in a peaceful and happy place.

Changing your eating habits and increasing your omega-3 oil intake with be just as good for you. You might want to consider that increasing the omega-3s is also associated with better heart health, fewer strokes, and less Alzheimer's disease. Other stress-reducing vitamins are of a very minor value, but time-release vitamin C (like, Ester-C™) does seem to improve mood, in one study.

Increase your daily exercise, if you can, and try to exercise in a way that brings you a peaceful and happy feeling. I personally like riding bicycles and walking. If your knees are healthy, jogging can be very enjoyable. While you exercise, nurture happy feelings. Review the things in your life that you do like, and want to see continue. Think of things that bless your life. Be glad you are living on a beautiful world like ours.

Chapter Five

Anger and Resentment

When one's expectations are reduced to zero, one can truly appreciate what one does have.
    – Stephen Hawking

A s you work on major triggers to anger, it may occur to you that smaller versions of anger are also present, namely 'resentment.' Do small injustices bother you? Are you irritated easily by unfairness?

Small irritations make us more likely to respond with anger to large things. Even a small resentment is a way of making our temper a hair-trigger. If you want an anger-free life, is it worth your while to deal with resentment? Are you able to rise to the challenge? Are you able to become intolerant of your own intolerance? Can you see that there is something much more important than resenting?

What good is it? What causes it?

Reflect on how useful it is for you to feel irritated. What is the advantage? Doesn't it just separate you from others, reduce the love and warmth and replace it with accusation?

Resentment and irritation seem to arise from a common habit of *expectations*. We expect more than we get, and we *criticize / judge* the person or circumstance. That may take the form of words such as 'things *should be different*,' or 'You *should do* this differently.' The words you would notice yourself saying would include 'should,' 'ought,' 'need to' and similar imperatives.

The underlying theory that drives people to resentment seems to be that if things were as we want them to be, then we would be happy. People should be making us happy, so we feel justified in criticizing them. We seldom ponder or contemplate this underlying theory. Is it true, that if things are as we want them, we will be happy? What do you really think about that?

Temporary Happiness

Have you ever noticed that when things are as we wish, we are in fact satisfied for a while? Do you notice that after a time, we begin to feel unhappy again? Researchers in happiness, such as David Myers and his colleagues, find that people become used to things being 'perfect' and tend to return to their original level of happiness. People who suddenly win a great deal of money in a lottery are temporarily happier. That lasts usually for a short time, less than six months. Then they return to their previous level of happiness.

Myers studied a woman who had barely been making ends meet. She was unhappy. In fact, the only happiness she ever had was buying one lottery ticket per week for the Illinois lottery. Then she felt happy, at least for a few minutes.

Then she won! She won big, over $20 million, and she was happy. She bought a nice home in a fancy part of town, she bought a new Jaguar, she enrolled her two sons in a fancy private school. She really was happy.

Within six months, she was in psychotherapy, with an expensive therapist. The diagnosis? Depression! She had returned to her previous level of happiness.

By way of contrast, studies of persons who had become paraplegic and were confined to a wheelchair found that within a year or so, the disabled person's level of happiness is about what it was before the accident that took his ability to walk. Temporarily it is true that there is great sorrow. But it is only temporary.

If you are a new professor, the most important thing is to get tenure. It is the key to keeping your job. New professors estimated that not getting tenure would be devastating and that it would permanently affect their lives.

The ones who did not get tenure were unhappy. But not for long. Within a year, they were just as happy as the professors who had gotten tenure.

That means that outside things don't really affect our happiness *in the long run*. For the short run, we are temporarily happier if we get what we want. In the long run, our happiness is probably something set from birth or early childhood.

If you want to be happier, you have to do something to change your innate level of happiness. You cannot look to others to make that long-run change in your happiness level.

What can we do? We can cultivate positive emotions, we can achieve joy when we embrace the goal of changing our happiness level from the inside out.

But we can never get to happiness by criticizing others. We cannot be happier from getting others to give us what we want. The happiness must be an "inside job." So let's think together about what might make that "inside job" work for you.

Costs of Criticizing

What does criticizing do to your relationships? What might you be missing?

Can you think of a time when you were completely happy and satisfied with your life? If not, perhaps you are in a criticism and irritation habit. If you look back and see disappointments in your life, could you imagine that perhaps, just perhaps you are unhappy because of the habit of irritation?

You have been working on a diary, and you have been writing down things at the end of the day that you feel good about, things you want to have continue in your life. It is possible that you are already beginning to notice that some things simply don't irritate you quite as much.

You have been practicing some self-calming skills. The Autogenic Training in the appendix is a very useful way to do this. It is possible that already you are starting to feel less irritable.

But if you have a long history of criticizing and if people try to accommodate you, it is likely that they have been unwittingly training you to be a grouch! You are getting rewarded for criticizing and as a result, you will be at risk for doing more and more of that.

Short term and long term

If you want temporary happiness, criticizing others may help. If you want long-term happiness, you have to adopt a long-term strategy of changing what you think, rather than wanting the people in the world to change to meet your needs.

Psychologist Barbara Fredrickson of the University of Michigan has found that negative and positive emotions can be cultivated. She also finds that negative emotions (fear, resentment, anger . . . and so on) produce a <u>narrowing of attention</u> and result in primitive and instinctive behaviors. I like to think of anger as reducing my own IQ by about 20 or 30 points! If you are pretty smart, maybe this doesn't hurt you. But I can't afford to lose that many points; I <u>have</u> to stay positive or I will get pretty stupid!

Positive emotions, such as joy, interest, and contentment, produce learning, creativity, and growth. They are the opposite, they make us smarter. And Fredrickson also found that we can cultivate and learn to have positive emotions just as we can learn a new language or how to cook a gourmet meal.

How does that apply to your relationship? What if you decided that criticizing others wasn't your job? In the movie, *Joe Versus the Volcano*, the character Angelica (Meg Ryan) asks Joe (Tom Hanks), "Didja ever think about suicide?" Joe is horrified and asks her why she would think of that. She replies, "Why not?"

"Well," Joe responds, "some things take care of themselves. *Some things just aren't our business.*" (Italics added)

Maybe it isn't your business to make other people change. Maybe your job is different. Criticism as a habit tells us that our job is to make other people change to meet our preferences. What if you decided that your job was to enjoy others, even when they aren't that easy to enjoy? Mark Twain once said that Wagner's music is better than it sounds. I suppose that might mean that if one were to study Wagner, one would enjoy his music more. So it is in your work and family. If you study enjoying others, you will find ways to do that.

Try this:

So how do we do it? There are many ways to cultivate certain emotions, but one simple way is to notice when we have them. Try this experiment: Keep a diary of the peak emotions you feel every day. Since everyone has ups and downs in their emotions, it should be rather easy for you to notice when you feel slightly better than usual. Put a name on the emotion, such as 'contentment' or 'pride' or 'appreciation.' Then write down what kinds of thoughts were going through your mind when you noticed the feeling. Jot down every time your emotions are a bit more positive, and you will soon notice your feelings becoming much more positive on a regular basis.

Use the diary to desensitize yourself to triggers by finding higher ways to see things that irritate you. What is good about them? How are they actually to your advantage?

Use the diary to track your own progress. When you find that something is less irritating, write about that with some satisfaction. Allow yourself to be pleased with your own progress. When you feel happy or peaceful, write about how you achieved that.

Take the credit! Realize that you are establishing new thinking habits and as you do that, your feelings are changing. You are doing that! It isn't just happening, it is your own achievement. Too often, people who are angry, or perfectionistic, tend to be as rough on themselves as they are on other people. If you are self-blaming, if you are judgmental about yourself as angry people are about other people, then you have to decide to give that up, just as angry people have to decide to give up the anger response.

Here is a quote on anger from the best author of contemporary fantasy / science fiction:

"Sarai knew that Qira would do it, and she also knew that getting mad at Qira would only make it worse, but it's not like you could stop being angry, it just filled you up and you couldn't think about anything else until you either used up the anger or something else happened to take your mind off it."

– Orson Scott Card, *Sarah*.

By cultivating positive emotions, you will find that there are many things that take your mind off the anger, and you are angry / resentful / negative less and less. Learning to be in command of your own mind is the best and most important task you will ever achieve in this life, and I hope this small chapter will be of some help in that quest.

Fortunately we can also develop habits of calm and courage when 'under fire,' so to speak. When a boss or a spouse is chronically angry, it is only natural we will either feel angry or fearful. What is the opposite of fear? Perhaps it is calm and peace. Perhaps 'confidence' comes to mind. I don't mean a belief that you will win, but rather that all will be well, at least in the long run.

You might want to try to take a longer view. "He is angry now, but he always gets over it. I can ride this out, and it will probably change soon."

You might want to cultivate a broader view. "He is probably just insecure, and uses anger to hide that from himself. I need to take a larger view of this."

You might even see it as a benefit to yourself! "When he gets angry, it is a perfect time for me to cultivate a feeling of confidence. If he didn't get angry, I would never be able to practice that confident feeling!"

Notice and cultivate those peaceful or confident feelings. Then your mind will be able to see possibilities you have never seen, and you will consider and explore pathways you have never trod.

"Resentment is like drinking poison and then hoping it will kill your enemies."

– Nelson Mandela,, actually quoting Confucius.

Chapter Six

Anger Versus Compassion

> A human being is part of a whole, called by us the Universe, a part limited in time and space. He experiences himself, his thoughts and feelings, as something separated from the rest-- a kind of optical delusion of his consciousness. This delusion is a kind of prison for us, restricting us to our personal desires and to affection for a few persons nearest us. Our task must be to free ourselves from this prison by widening our circles of compassion to embrace all living creatures and the whole of nature in its beauty.
> – Albert Einstein

I have been suggesting positive emotions as a great antidote to anger. Now lets discuss the most positive emotion for that, compassion. When we practice compassion, we are developing a habit of seeing all behavior in a sympathetic way.

There are two parts to compassion. First, we have to be able to imagine how other people feel, how they might experience themselves and the world. This is the empathy portion.

Second, we then have a desire to relieve the suffering of others. These two parts - empathy and a wish to remove suffering - are keys. And they are also keys for feeling much happier than you ever thought was possible.

Compassion means you choose to view other people as like yourself, as having the best of intentions, and as perhaps doing negative or bad things out of ignorance or misunderstanding. It means we decide to attribute good motives and desires to all others. It means you make a decision to cultivate a tender and understanding approach to those who irritate you. Compassion means you have empathy for the suffering of others, and you wish to relieve that suffering.

For example, you are driving in a sensible way and someone speeds by you and creates a dangerous situation. Compassion would cause us to look at that behavior with some sympathy, such as, "That poor guy must really be in a hurry! I hope nothing bad happens to him!"

You actually might disagree. In fact, you may secretly hope something bad does happen to him! He has irritated you. As you know now, to live anger-free means we have to decide to deal immediately with irritations. Compassion is a decision. Here are some steps I find helps us to carry out that decision.

Compassion for Self

> "If you want others to be happy, practice compassion. If you want to be happy, practice compassion."
> – The Dalai Lama

First, have some compassion for yourself. It is only natural for you to feel irritated or bothered, it is not bad, it is understandable. Then notice what is the feeling behind the irritation. Perhaps it is fear. Perhaps it is a feeling of inferiority. Whatever it is, have a sense of compassion for that feeling behind the irritation.

Soothe yourself. Recognize it is quite understandable that you feel the vulnerable feeling, such as fear or inferiority.

Talk supportively to yourself. Speak soothing words in your mind. "I do the best I know how at the time. I may not be perfect, but my heart is in the right place. I want the best for other people." It is not your job to chastise and criticize yourself. It doesn't work, and you are not objective enough to fairly judge yourself. Every human being makes mistakes. The wise thing is to try to learn from them and move on.

Many people will *ruminate* about mistakes, run them over and over in their own minds. Usually there will be a running commentary about what a terrible thing that was that they did and how stupid and worthless they are for doing that. They think they are learning from that, saying 'I shouldn't have done this, I should never have done that.' They think they can help themselves be wiser by such negative self-talk.

They are wrong.

Research into people who do such *counter-factual* (i.e., against the facts) thinking actually do not learn or grow as fast as people who think they did something wrong, try to set it right, and then move on. They get stuck and paradoxically make the same kinds of mistakes over and over again. People who simply recognize, "Oh, I did that wrong, it was a mistake. Oh, well, I did the best I could." seem to correct mistakes much faster. I know this may seem completely counter-intuitive to you. I recognize what I am saying may seem radical and irresponsible. All I can say is that it does work.

Compassion might be called a key positive emotion. Feeling compassion for others will be a tremendous advantage in having a peaceful and happy life. Start with you. If you practice it with yourself, you can practice it with others.

Forgiveness

To forgive is to set a prisoner free and discover that the prisoner
was you.
– Lewis B. Smedes

One challenge to compassion is resentment. Someone has hurt
you. You are angry with that person. You wish that person could
suffer as you have suffered. This is the opposite of compassion.

But realistically, it is likely you do feel resentment. People do
hurt us and damage us. It is completely understandable that we would
have some genuine anger and resentment.

So here you are: On the one hand, you want to be happy. On the
other hand, you have been hurt, and you are angry about that. Such
feelings make you suffer, but it is very hart to let go of them. What
shall we do?

In the past few years, psychologists have studied these feelings
and have found that forgiveness is a skill that some people have to
keep themselves from suffering. People who practice the skill of
forgiveness on a regular basis are clearly more happy, more friendly
and warm, and more successful. They may feel pain but not hurt. That
means that they do not keep track of the pain. They release it. They
do not dwell on it, so they do not hurt. The pain passes them quickly.

Should we forgive people if they ask our pardon? Well, put
yourself in their shoes. If you knew you had done something wrong,
you would want people to forgive you, would you not? So to the
extent that you can, that kind of forgiveness is a good idea.

Be Wise

That doesn't mean you would trust the person who hurt you. After all, forgiveness cleanses your own heart and mind. It lays down a burden and helps you to feel lighter. But trust is a different issue altogether. The person may not be trustworthy. So just because you were to forgive would not mean you would trust. In fact, trust might be very unwise.

Your forgiveness, in a way, is for your benefit. Trust would be for the other person's benefit. Let them earn that. If not, then guard your own safety as carefully as you work to forgive.

Forgiveness is a lifestyle, but it isn't a foolish one.

Keys to Forgiving

The weak can never forgive. Forgiveness is the attribute of the strong.
    – Mahatma Gandhi

Let's talk about a method. In the past few years, psychologists have studied forgiveness and found several pathways. I am proposing you use Dr. Everett Worthington's five step forgiveness method. It isn't necessarily the best. It isn't the worst. It works for me and for most people. If you find a better way, wonderful!

He suggests you think of forgiveness as a pyramid one climbs. There are five steps to his pyramid, which you can remember by the word "**REACH**." I suggest you write a response to each of the five steps in your journal or diary. Don't go through this quickly but rather give your mind and heart time to adjust to the idea of forgiveness.

R: Recall the pain and hurt you have suffered. True forgiveness comes when we actually have an injury to forgive, and you owe yourself the respect of acknowledging the pain. Write about it. Describe it. Let the feelings out onto the paper. Realistically look at the hurt and now let yourself wish for a relief of the pain from those feelings. Don't blame the other person, but rather just focus on your own goal of peace and forgiveness.

E: Empathize with the perpetrator of your hurt. This is a very hard, step, but doable. Write about what may have motivated that person to hurt you. Try to put yourself in the shoes of that other person. Write a letter to yourself as if you were the other person and you were trying to explain your acts. What could have motivated that person to harm you? What kinds of thoughts and beliefs might that person have? What kinds of emotions was he or she experiencing? Think of times when you believed something foolish, felt some strong, destructive emotion. Try to see the world through the eyes of your enemy. Write it down.

A: Altruistic Gift. The altruistic gift of forgiveness means that you forgive not because the person deserves it but rather because you have made some mistakes in your own life and would hope others would forgive you. Altruism means practicing the golden rule, do unto others as you would wish they would do unto you.

Worthington points out that perhaps you harmed or offended a friend, a parent, or a partner who later forgave you? Didn't you feel guilty? Then reflect on how you felt when you were forgiven. People say, "I felt free. I felt a burden was lifted."Forgiveness relieves guilt. By recalling your own guilt and the gratitude over being forgiven, you will sense a desire to give that gift of freedom to the person who hurt you. Write in your journal about how you want forgiveness yourself, and how you give because you wish to have that given to you.

In altruism we believe that we help ourselves by helping others. Write in this letter how you hope to do yourself some good by forgiving the other person.

C: Commit to yourself that you will forgive. Promise yourself that you will. **Certify** that you have forgiven. Make an actual **certificate** or letter attesting to your forgiveness of the other person. Tell others that you have forgiven the person you were angry with, and show them the certificate. You do not have to show the perpetrator the certificate. That may or may not be wise. Always be wise.

Generally one would not have to tell the person who has done real damage that he or she has been forgiven. If it is someone who merely hurt some feelings, perhaps feeling justified, then you might want to let them know you forgive them. Even better, you might want to ask their forgiveness. You have nurtured some harsh feelings toward that person, ruminating on how you were hurt. Ask forgiveness for that.

But again, be wise, very wise.

H: Hold on to the forgiveness. When the memories come back – and naturally enough, they will come back – just recall the Certificate of Forgiveness, and remind yourself that you have already forgiven that. **Help** yourself by writing about how you have remembered that you have already forgiven.

Worthington suggests that some hurts will take several trips up the pyramid. Perhaps that will be true for you too. I have come to think that forgiveness is more a way of life than a single event. Like eating healthy food or exercise, it just takes persistence and perseverance.

Sometimes people fear forgiving an evil person because they very well might harm them again. This is a sensible position to take. Being forgiving doesn't mean you have to be foolish. If the angry person hasn't changed his ways, you would be silly to let your forgiveness make you do something risky. That is not it. Forgiveness is a spiritual approach to life, not a silly one. Do it because it makes the whole world a better place, and makes your own heart a better place for you to live.

Just as we all need to forgive, we all need forgiveness. St. Paul says in the Bible that we all are sinners and come short of the glory of God. To me, that is a comforting thought. It means I can look at every person in the world with compassion and understanding. From the greatest to the least, we are all human and we all make mistakes. Let us embrace the life of forgiveness.

I often have people object to this idea. They believe the angry person should suffer for the pain he has put his employees or his family or his friends through. These people accuse me of letting the angry person off the hook.

There may be some truth to that. All I can say is that confronting the angry person just makes them all the more angry. After all, the angry person is very good at being angry, and when we are under stress, we do what is familiar to us.

That doesn't mean that people are not responsible. If you broke it, you have to fix it. I am not going to fix your mistakes and pick up after your temper tantrums, and you shouldn't do that for anyone either. But it does help us to cultivate compassion and forgiveness in yourself, not to let people off the hook, but so that you will be at your most creative and intelligent when dealing with an angry person. Forgiveness accomplishes that.

So I am asking you - a person dealing with an angry person - to try to find some compassion or at least tolerance and patience. That angry person doesn't deserve it. No argument there. But the compassion and the patience work better.

Compassion for Others

Recognize that the other person is probably just caught up in their own problems and insecurities and they don't really recognize how much problem they are causing. Extend a sense of understanding and compassion to that person.

Make a decision: It is better for me to forgive this person. I deserve to live a life of peace and happiness, and that can only come through forgiveness.

Speak soothing words in your own mind about the bad situation. This is a chance to practice compassion. If you are a religious person, turn it over to the higher power that you respect and worship. Say in your mind, "Dear God, please take care of this. I turn it over to You and ask You to apply Your wisdom and compassion to this person."

This is not a one-time change but something you must do over and over again. In my neighborhood we have a pesky weed called the field bindweed, or wild morning glory. The way we get rid of it is to hoe it off at the surface all summer long. By the time fall comes, the deep roots have lost most of their strength and often the weed will die during the winter. Like a perennial weed that must be hoed over and over again, each time you turn something over you become calmer and stronger, and the angry or hurt thought becomes weaker.

Reverse the Behavior

As you work with compassion, you will become more aware of the small behaviors that go along with irritation.

As you feel an increase in compassion, you will naturally be less controlled by the impulse associated with irritation. Become aware of what your tendency is when you feel irritated. Perhaps it is an angry word, perhaps it is a clenching of the jaw.

Now take that impulse and reverse it. Whatever you are aware of feeling, such as an urge to strike out, then reverse it and do the opposite. A striking out becomes an affectionate touch. A curse becomes a blessing. "Teaching a lesson" becomes helping the other person deal with consequences.

The more you practice these principles – feel compassion for yourself, feel compassion for the other, and practice reversal of the behavior – the more happy and peaceful you will feel.

You will discover that your life is better for it.

Try it and see. Use your diary to write down compassionate ways to see people who are making you angry. (And, remember to start with writing compassion toward yourself!) Make your best effort to see those new views as helpful to your. Put your heart into it! After all, if you don't find that this causes you to feel peaceful and happy, you can always go back to being irritated!

But I don't think you will. I think you will find it a better way to live.

Let me repeat myself. People who have to cope with the angry person will object to this emphasis on compassion. "He doesn't deserve compassion!" they will insist.

And of course, they are right. They - the angry people of this world - really don't. And that is exactly the core of compassion. It is a gift, a gift that is motivated by a decision to be compassionate. It isn't something that people have to earn. In fact, if they earn a good feeling, we wouldn't call the feeling we have toward them 'compassion' but rather something else.

If they earn a good feeling, it might be admiration we feel, or approval, or even awe. But it is not compassion. They key to compassion is a desire we have within ourselves to make the life of another person better. Like Mother Teresa going to the slums of Calcutta, we are doing it because we have simply decided that compassion counts.

I am probably better off in this world than I deserve to be, especially when I read about people fighting each other in the Sudan, people living lives of poverty and despair in the rural areas of China, people in North Korea starving and dying because of the madness of their leaders.

Do I deserve what I have? Most of it, I was simply born into. I was raised in a country that gave me second and third chances. I was nurtured in a country that allowed anyone who wants to, a chance to attend college. I live in a country that allows me to have clear title to property, title that allows me access to credit, which in turn I can use to form my own business. I live in a country where the rule of law, not the whims of man, is paramount. I didn't deserve these things, neither did you. We all get more blessings than we deserve.

So why not decide to bless the lives of others by a commitment to compassion? Does he - the angry person - deserve your compassion? Of course not. That is the beauty of it!

Chapter Seven

Just a Second . . .

> Between the event and the reaction is an incredibly brief moment. We call that moment 'freedom.'
> – the Author

L et's talk about time. When you are hit by an event that triggers anger in you, there is a very brief time during which you can make a choice of calm or anger. Skills at recognizing this brief moment help you to reclaim yourself from anger's grasp.

Our Vital Switch

The amygdala is the brain's switch. As you now know, there are actually two; one on each side of the head, deep inside, and located about half way between the corner of the eye and the ear. This small, almond-shaped area samples whatever is coming in your eyes and your ears, looking for dangers.

People who are either very easily frightened or who are easily angered have amygdalas that are too reactive. They are like the brain of a wild animal, all fight and flight. Bear in mind, then, that you can tame a wild animal. I have done it myself. All it takes is some consistency and patience. Keep working, and you will tame the amygdala.

Just a word here: Let me remind you that the amygdala is only one short nerve cell away from the eyes and the ears. The amygdala actually perceives sights and sounds sooner than your conscious mind. Suddenly seeing a snake coiled up, you react with fear. What you don't realize is that the fear shift started up to a half a second before your conscious mind had a chance to notice the snake.

Because the amygdala is so small, its' ability to figure out a complicated stimulus is very limited. If something looks sort of like a past event where you felt insecure and coped with anger, you will get a shift of energy away from the highest levels of the brain and toward the reptile center. You can often actually feel the energy drain away from your clear thinking and toward hot thoughts driven by angry instincts.

As that energy drains away, you still have a moment to seize control. A quick deep breath, followed by a slow exhale, will help. Then you want to *distract* yourself. Some tools for that are to quickly count backwards by 3's from a number like 47. That will take some concentration!

Another good trick is to count backward in a foreign language, one you don't know very well.

Another anger-defeating trick is to recall the names of some of the children in your class in elementary school. Perhaps you can try to recall the names of children sitting in your row in sixth grade. Any difficult mental problem will quickly calm you down.

Quick! What are the names of the Seven Dwarfs?

What was Bambi's mother's name?

Where did you hide important things when you were a child?

Compassionate self-talk will help. "It is normal to feel some anger, but I am capable of handling this. I don't need to do anything right now about that. It is worthwhile for me to stop and think."

Above all, don't do anything! Wait. You are upset, angry. This is a time for quiet. This is a time to use the instinctive *freeze* reaction. Just wait and let the feeling pass. Recall some of these mind-stimulating exercises in the book. But wait. Soon your reason will return and you will be able to function much better!

A Friendly Warning

Most important thought: Please recognize that the amygdala's snatching power from the higher brain is something that has kept humans alive in dangerous, primitive conditions. Our parents are those who reacted with quick fear or anger. Our more sloth-like brothers and sisters were eaten by cave bears and saber-toothed tigers! They didn't pass on their genes.

That means that when the rear part of the amygdala flairs, we feel an *almost* undeniable desire to DO SOMETHING! In other words, the hardest thing to do is the right thing to do in our civilized society. You really don't need to kill and eat your boss when he yells at you. It just feels like that.

So the rule of anger is, "don't say anything; don't do anything until you can calm down." But it is a very hard rule. You have to consciously recognize and be convinced that it is a very good rule, because it contradicts our instinctive wiring. You have to really believe that you don't think clearly when you are angry.

That's why yelling and raging when we are angry feels so right at the time, even though later on we can see that was a terribly foolish thing to do. Our brains are wired that way, and it is natural. We want to become, if you will, <u>supernatural</u>! Our natural self is wonderfully adapted for living in a kill-and-eat world. We want more! We want to be better than Mother Nature designed us to be!

EXERCISE YOUR BRAIN

Vividly recall a recent time when you felt angry. Try to recall the exact circumstances.

Now as you start to feel the anger, begin to calm and tame your wild amygdala. Try one of the exercises suggested above. Physically relax, choose compassion, see it anew.

Imagine yourself quickly intervening to achieve calm. Practice that five or ten times. If you can do that once a day, you will make some significant progress.

If you cannot achieve calm, then at least imagine yourself doing nothing until the feeling passes. Simply practice using the moment of freedom to chose to wait. Imagine what would happen next. How would it help?

Enter your progress in your journal.

Take A Break

Have you ever been in an argument where things scale up? You both get more and more angry and soon there are very ugly things being said?

The instincts we have of "DO SOMETHING!" when we are angry prevents the most helpful thing we could do.

Walk away for a half hour.

Sometimes one person will try to walk away from an argument but the other person won't let that happen. "No, stay here and settle this!" is the demand.

It won't work.

Once you are angry, your own lack of intelligence prevents the brain from coming up with a real solution. Your thinking is rigid and stereotyped. You are not creative.

But if you could walk around for thirty minutes or so, isn't there a possibility that you could calm down?

John Gottman is a marriage researcher who has pointed out that freezing out the other person may be the most upsetting and damaging thing a spouse can do. Perhaps if you would like to walk away for a while, your partner instinctively recognizes that as like some kind of freezing out. You no longer care.

One way to get someone to care is to get them mad at you. It is a cheap and reliable way to raise emotions. So you can see a kind of primitive wisdom in the demand, "No, you stay here and finish this."

So the way you frame this is going to make all the difference in the world. To convey the message, "Oh, forget it, I am out of here." is exactly the trigger for panic and rage in the other person.

What about a more thoughtful message: "I am pretty steamed and I know I am kind of stupid when I am upset. I need to calm down so that I can think this through. I'd like to walk around, cool down, and come back here in thirty or forty minutes. Maybe by then I won't be so irrational."

If that could be your message, it may make the difference.

You may also be caught up in this idea that "we have to keep talking until we finish this." Sometimes, frankly, the less angry person feels so desperate to make some kind of progress that they fall into this trap.

Don't believe it. Talking with each other when you are angry is not going to get you anywhere. It may feel deceptively important.

You might want to simply study that feeling. Relable it: "That feeling doesn't tell me what I should do. I can't trust that feeling because I know I am not as intelligent when I am upset and feeling desperate. I cannot trust my own feelings now.

Then take a walk (assuring your partner, of course, that you are not freezing him or her out, you are just trying to clear your head). Do some higher thinking, such as reviewing the big picture, or trying to recall some compassion and gratitude for your partner.

It will make a big difference.

Calming Self Talk

While you are walking around, I think you will notice how the brain likes to replay the triggers. That would keep the anger at a high pitch, of course, and you'd come back from your walk just as angry as when you left.

Instead of ruminating on the things your partner did wrong, how about having some compassion for yourself?

After all, it is pretty miserable to feel angry, isn't it? Oh, I know how seductive the feeling of anger is. We feel that we are *RIGHT* and justified. But look below the surface. Can you feel how tense you are? Can you feel how uneven your breathing is? How does your heart feel? Is it racing or pounding?

If you had a best friend walking with you, helping you calm down, what would he say? Perhaps, "Look this isn't that big of a deal. It really isn't going to matter in a month, is it? Wouldn't you feel better and more clear-headed if you were to calm down? Yes, he upsets you, and probably you upset him! Both of you could do some calming down. Why not start with yourself?"

Whatever your friend might say, that could be the sort of thing you would say to yourself.

Now as soon as you start to calm down, become mindful of your setting. If it were during the evening or night, notice how the world starts to quiet down. Notice the play of light and dark. Notice the temperature on your skin. Become aware of all you can. That tends to calms us down fairly well.

Finally, shift toward compassion for your partner. You have felt anger and fear, so you know how that feels. Your partner is suffering from those same feelings. Wouldn't you like to relieve those painful feelings? Wouldn't you like to see peace and harmony in your partner's eyes?

Be sure and document your progress in your journal.

Are you getting better at compassion? Each time you choose that road, you are taming the wild amygdala. You are transcending your natural self and becoming 'super-natural.' Write about your progress in your journal. Track your own feelings of compassion and their effect on you.

This chapter works just as well for you as it does for your partner. The same "time out" homework works there too. You can try a time out walk if you are arguing. You can say with just as must truth that you are also less intelligent and more irrational when you are angry. You also need all your insight and intelligence. You also can benefit from exercising compassion.

Journal your results.

Chapter Eight

Having Impact: Develop Positive Influence

Ships that pass in the night and speak each other in passing;
Only a signal shown and a distant voice in the darkness;
So on the ocean of life we pass and speak one another,
Only a look and a voice; then darkness again and a silence.
   – Henry Wadsworth Longfellow

Perhaps we are on the same page, so to speak, and you are beginning to question whether Anger is really the friend it tries to make you think. Perhaps this is not a friend at all, perhaps it is a habit that costs a lot and actually makes things in your life worse. But, as we discussed earlier, giving up something familiar is frightening. It makes good sense for you to hesitate to really challenge the anger habit. You may believe that you will have no impact on others, that they will just ignore you, and you will be powerless.

If I were Anger and I didn't want you to kick me out of your life, that is exactly the threat I would play against you. I would try to convince you, "Oh, I may not be perfect, but you would be lost without me! Everyone would disrespect you! It would be awful!"

Would you be?

Am I Powerless Without Anger?

That is a perfectly good question. We do not want to be powerless. People need to have an impact on the world. It is just how we are made. When you were just a little baby, making things happen by yourself was one of your great pleasures. So it is absolutely vital that you have influence and impact on others. This chapter will cover the principle of positive power.

Why People Change

When we talk about how you can have influence on people, it will help you to understand some basic information about leadership. Psychologists at the University of New York at Binghamton, Dr. Bernard Bass and Dr. Bruce Avolio, have studied all kinds of leaders, successful ones and failures. Ironically, they found clearly that among the least effective leaders were those who primarily used anger and intimidation to have an influence on others. Usually such leaders have a negative influence. In other words, the workers would perform better without that manager.

So if Anger is whispering in your ear that without it, you will be powerless, steal a page from Bass and Avolio, and tell Anger that is a lie. In fact, you will be more influential without it!

Great leaders are able to help people achieve high levels of performance. They do this with positive sources of influence:

1. **Caring - love - individual concern**. Great leaders make people around them feel cared about, appreciated, and respected. We work hard for people who care; people don't care how much you know until they know how much you care.

2. **Personal example**: Great leaders walk the walk, and do what they ask others to do. If salary cutbacks are necessary, the excellent leader takes the first hit. If hard work is called for, the extraordinary leader works as hard as anyone.

3. **Self-interest**: Great leaders appeal to our own self-interest. They tell us that the vision is important, the goal is worthy. They tell us that we can help achieve positive goals. They make us see how we can

help.

We see the vision, we want to be part of the winning team. Everyone wants to be on the winning side!

4. **Challenge and mastery of difficulty**: Great leaders present difficult challenges and give us feedback about how we are doing. They appeal to our intelligence and help us discover better ways to do things. They talk about the problems, but they don't solve them for us. They appeal to us to use our own intelligence and insight. They appreciate it when we do.

5. **Self-disclosure**: Positive leaders share their inner thoughts and feelings. They don't pretend to be what they are not; they are more of who they really are. They share embarrassing things about themselves. They apologize for mistakes or failures. They admit it when they are being selfish or short-sighted. It may seem paradoxical to you, but a great leader is first to admit her or his mistakes. And that is what makes people love them. It is far easier to like someone who is fallible and human that to like a leader that makes us feel inferior.

Psychologists have found that many leaders are quick to anger. They influence people by their sharpness and irritability. Leadership research shows convincingly that power derived from anger is false power. Power from anger will never touch the other person's heart. They will only obey as long as you are watching. After a while, you have no time to do anything except to watch. As soon as you are out of sight, people will go back to doing what they wanted.

The best leaders energize and inspire. The mediocre ones simply threaten. Do you want to be mediocre or be the best?

The Folly of Force

As I write this, American forces in Iraq have not found the

weapons of mass destruction that were thought by the United Nations to exist. Every intelligence service in the free world believed they were there. But they are not! Many are wondering why. The other day I read a small item that might explain it. Intelligence documents from pre-war Iraq seem to address this mystery.

It seems that Saddam Hussain had a great enthusiasm for any program of weapons, and would throw lots of money at those programs. However, his follow-up was not good. Scientists were possibly taking money for programs that didn't really exist. The WMDs might have been bureaucratic boondoggle, imaginary weapons that never got stockpiled. Saddam may have thought he had them and he really didn't!

Authoritarian governments always have that problem. They are inherently terribly inefficient, because they are based on force. There was an old joke in the Soviet Union that the regime was based on pretense. The workers would say, "We pretend to work, and they pretend to pay us."

So even if this explanation for the missing WMDs doesn't turn out to be true, the principle is a true one. Force can never govern the human spirit.

The Real Source of Power

Only love can touch the heart. True power comes not from anger and hate, it comes from love. The most powerful force in human society is love. The greatest achievements of all time are based on it.

If you give up anger, you are opening up the possibility of achieving these kinds of influence, influence that will last a long time and motivate people to do their best long after you have left the scene. That is real power, not the phony and illusory power that anger delivers. Oh, anger may promise power and long-lasting results, but it never can deliver! Talk back to those false promises! Don't let the promises of anger rob you of true influence. Allow me to offer some proof.

What is the secret behind individuals who are resilient and bounce back from setbacks quickly? What about marriages that seem to sail through the storms of life, with both persons happy and content? What is the secret of business teams that excel and exceed expectations?

As it turns out, there is a common denominator. It is the Positive to Negative ratio.

Deeply wired into our brains is an automatic judging process, distinguishing positive / negative. Every baby knows the difference between pain and pleasure, sweet and sour, harsh and gentle. As adults it's the same. Rich, we are told, is better than poor, and happy is good while sad is bad. Healthy is good, sickness is bad. Our brains are designed to make those judgements.

We now know that anything negative has a large impact on our brain. Negative is a message of "stop, danger, watch out!" Negative disorganizes our efforts. It helps us know when something is not working. Negative shifts physical energy away from maintenance and immunity toward fight or flight.

Positive tells us, "you are OK, keep up the good work, things are going well." It tells us to create, invent, and discover, because it is safe to explore. Positive shifts physical energy to immunity, learning, and growing.

Positive keeps you healthy: In one recent study, Erik Giltay in the Netherlands found that men between the ages of 65 and 84 are at a greater or lesser risk of heart attack based only on how optimistic they are. Men who were in the top third of optimism had about half the number of heart attacks over a fifteen year period than men who were at the bottom third.

In another study, people recovering from a heart attack were asked from time to time to write down what they were thinking. Those diaries were scored for positive and negative feelings. Those who had a 1:1 ratio of positive to negative thoughts and feelings were far more likely to have other heart attacks and/or die than those who had a 4:1 or 5:1 ratio of positive to negative.

Positive helps marriage: James Gottman has studied marriages and finds something similar. Gottman asked married couples to come to his lab and have conversations. When the positive-to-negative ratios were about 4:1 or 5:1, those marriages succeeded. But when the ratios were around 1:1, the marriages were very likely to end in divorce.

Positive means profit: In Brazil, Marcial Losada studied business teams that were either languishing or flourishing. What he discovered was remarkably similar. Teams have to face and deal with problems, but the flouishing teams had a positive:negative ratio of 5.6 to one. Teams that were only partially productive had a ratio of 1.8 to one. And the languishing teams, where little productive work was getting done, had a ratio of .4 to one!

Why would this be? I think perhaps it is because life is a challenge, and to meet that challenge, we must believe that we can succeed. When our thinking and feeling have a mostly positive ratio, our communication will reflect that, and both we and the people around us succeed. When we are mostly positive, we don't give up, we keep trying to find pathways to success.

But we are often rewarded for discovering and dealing with problems. Sometimes we do that through negativity, responding with fear or anger. This can be dangerous and create an attitude oriented toward problems and not toward solutions. We have to bear in mind that negativity takes it toll on us, and we have to balance negative events out, according to importance research by Losada and Barbara Fredrickson, professor of psychology at the University of North Carolina. Since we now know that negative events "weigh more" so to speak (they have a more drastic impact on us), we have to put several positive events on the scale for balance. If it were a bank balance, the average negative is $100 withdrawal, and the average positive is about a $20 to $35 deposit. It turns out that, according to the Fredrickson and Losada work, you move from languishing to flourishing when the positive ratio is 2.9:1. Around 5:1 seems to be optimal, and above that, there is probably too much positivity, it becomes unrealistic, and the health of the individual or group declines.

Now some negatives are not a $100 withdrawal. They are much more, perhaps $1000 or $10,000. If you were to hit someone, that may be a $10,000 withdrawal and paying it off at $20 per positive event is going to take a very long time.

Some relationships go bankrupt and that brings about divorce in a marriage or quitting a job. The relationship is so far in the hole that divorce seems like the only option.

Now you and I both know there is another option, namely that of forgiveness. But you are the only one who can forgive. If you think you can demand forgiveness of another person, then you haven't read this book very carefully! Forgiveness is for you to do, not something you can demand.

Homework Suggestion

Imagine you could take an emotional temperature of your environment. If warm is a higher temperature and cold is a lower one, what temperature rating would people around you give today? Would they feel your warmth, or would Anger make them feel cold? What would you do to warm up the environment? What can show genuine warmth to those around you?

Write down some thoughts about warming up your environment. Whether you show anger at work or at home, how would people around you know that you had experienced a change of heart? How would they know that you were letting true warmth and appreciation out?

Write down these thoughts and revisit them from time to time. Do they suggest the kind of person you really want to be?

Deep Listening: The Skill of Connection

One way you can reliably put more emotional currency into your relationship bank account is to improve your listening skills.

People like to be heard. To be heard helps reduce insecurity. It gives us a feeling of peace. And when someone really listens to us, we often discover something about ourselves. In this section I will explain two ways of listening and encourage you to try to listen better.

ANALYTIC LISTENING: This is the kind of listening we usually do. During Analytic Listening I am evaluating in my mind as I listen to you. I am busy judging and deciding what to say.

As a result, you don't feel *heard*. You may repeat yourself, or feel annoyed. Maybe I can even repeat back to you what I "heard" but it just doesn't feel like I listened to you. That is because when you are talking, I am guarding my heart. I am not letting what you say touch me. And you know it.

DEEP LISTENING: A rare talent. In deep listening, my mind is very quiet when I listen. My feeling is peaceful and curious. I don't take things personally, judge or decide or figure anything out. I don't try to remember anything. My mind is quiet and open. I let myself be touched.

As a result, you find you don't repeat yourself as much. You feel a connection. You are likely to say, "I don't know why, but I really felt you *heard* me." Your feelings will become more peaceful.

Let's compare the two.

ANALYTIC LISTENING

MOOD: More tense, distracted.

MIND: Busy with judgement and analysis; "If you say this, it probably means you also think that" Feeling of preoccupation.

MEMORY: Effort made to not forget anything, so while that is going on, the listening is distracted.
Fear that something might be forgotten.

CONVERSATION: Frequent interruptions, challenges, confrontations.

RESPONSE TO BLAME: The analytic listener tries to show how the speaker is wrong; sounds defensive and closed.

PROBLEM SOLVING: Effort to force one person to accept the other's solution. Feels win-lose to both sides: "I must win or at least I must not lose."

DEEP LISTENING

MOOD: Peaceful and curious

MIND: Thoughts are dropped rather than pursued. Any analysis is ignored and discarded. Feeling is inquisitive.

MEMORY: No effort is made to remember anything. There is a quiet assurance that the mind will provide whatever memories are needed without forcing it.

CONVERSATION: Mostly questions, interruptions only when the listener is confused and unclear. No confrontations or challenges.

RESPONSE TO BLAME: Curiosity, puzzled. May say things like, "You could be right about that."

PROBLEM SOLVING: Flashes of insight and intuition; there is a win-win attitude and solutions that would harm either party are simply rejected or ignored.

Did you notice that I didn't talk about active listening, the technique of repeating back what you heard the person say? This is a technique that was taught and was popular for years. The problem is that it is just a technique. Deep listening emphasizes what is in your heart. If you *intend* to hear me, the techniques are not important; if not, they don't matter. Only what is in your heart matters.

Speaking from your heart

After you have practiced deep listening, you are ready to begin speaking with power and influence. It will help you to make a study of *assertiveness*. Asserting yourself means to speak from your heart about what is important to you, but without threat or coercion. Assertiveness is speaking up with meaning but not with anger. Assertiveness takes the position that it is utterly unethical to force or coerce behavior. And, it is (as we have discussed in this book) also totally ineffective! It doesn't work!

When you assert yourself, you simply tell people what you want, why you think it is in their best interests, and leave them to choose. You speak about your interests, their interests, and the worthiness of your goals. You speak with power and energy about your vision. You speak like a leader, like a visionary. You speak from your deepest heart. Then you do let it go, and you leave those you are speaking to, to make their own decision.

If Anger has had your ear for years, the idea of leaving them to choose may seem illogical! "This is something that *has* to be done! There is no time for free and informed choice!"

In reality, there isn't enough time to *not* allow free choice. If your request is important, when you force it on people, they will promptly ignore it when you are out of sight. If it is so important, it deserves the process of allowing people to decide for themselves.

Assertiveness is a large and important topic. There are many good books on the subject, and they merit your study. The next chapter will briefly cover the topic. Have some faith that there is a better way, we know how to get there, and we can help you in the journey.

Often the angry person can be helped by your own ability to stay calm and peaceful in spite of the storms they create. I have seen good come from those moments of peace where the person the anger is directed against ask sincerely, "Do you really want me to fear and dislike you? Or can you find it in your heart to want me to respect and care about you? Your anger makes it very difficult for me to care about you; I become so afraid of you that I lose respect and care. I cannot believe that is what you really want."

In other words, the person who is targeted by the anger learns to speak from his or her heart. That person learns to show good leadership, to create a vital vision (a life of peace and harmony) and throw out an intellectual / moral challenge (anger making the vision impossible). Reflect on and write to yourself about your own leadership. Can you show those positive qualities of leadership? Can you increase your positive personal influence?

Chapter Nine

Assertiveness: *The Art of Speaking from Your Heart*

"While one person hesitates because he feels inferior, the other
is busy making mistakes and becoming superior."
– Henry C. Link

O ften we find people who cannot speak up about things that are
important. They feel inhibited or unable to tell people what
they want. Sometimes these people are just shy, something
that you are probably born with. Other times a person will have a
background that makes it hard to speak up. For example, maybe a
child growing up in a poor family wants a bicycle. He asks for what
he wants, but instead of understanding ("If I could get you one I
would, but we don't have the money.") he is criticized and attacked.
He learns to stifle his hopes and desires. He comes to expect that
speaking of his hopes will lead to disappointment.

Asserting Vs. Hiding

Sometimes if we cannot speak assertively, we become angry.
We then find that, temporarily, people will pay attention to us, so then
anger becomes our habit. We may get results with this, at least
temporarily. Being angry is not what I mean by assertiveness.
Assertiveness is not anger, it is respectful to you and others. You
show respect for yourself by speaking of what is important, and you
show respect for others by not forcing your will on them, by

recognizing their right to chose for themselves.

A recent study found that men who had physically abused their wives were actually less likely to speak up about what was in their hearts than men who had never had any physical confrontation. We have long known that anxiety and depression are higher in people who do not speak sincerely and frankly; now we know that violence is also more likely.

If you do not speak up about things important to you, then you will be more prone to becoming depressed or anxious. And if you do speak up, your levels of anxiety or depression will drop. You will be able to lead and influence others better. You will gain valuable feedback. It won't be easy, but it will help you to grow and become a better person.

Assertiveness Vs. Aggression

The opposite of hiding is to be overly aggressive. Perhaps you feel fearful of asserting yourself because true assertiveness allows the possibility that the other person may say 'no!' The fearful person cannot seem to bear that.

So sometimes we avoid saying what we really mean because we don't want to force people. But sometimes it is because we feel we *have* to win, to have people comply with our wishes.

While every person believes he or she has a good reason for wanting things his or her way, the plain fact of the matter is that these are preferences, and other people have different preferences.

Aggressive communication is based on anger, on the need to have things our own way, and it has all the drawbacks that anger has. People will go along with us but they resent it, or feel intimidated and cannot really love us or respect us. Only respect will bring forth respect and love, and if we don't practice that, we won't get it back. So not allowing people a choice is a form of anger that you will sometime pay a high price for, in one way or another.

A Better Way

The following exercise helps people speak up about things that are near and dear to their hearts, and helps them to become a better communicator.

There is someone you should talk to. It is probably the person who is the most difficult for you to communicate with, for one reason or another. When you start to talk to that person, you may find you freeze up or feel tongue tied. Or perhaps you become too angry and you can't speak truthfully. (People never speak the truth when angry, because their mind is unable to know the truth. Instead you speak words of exaggeration and anger. Only from the calm mind can one speak what is in one's heart.)

There are good reasons why you cannot speak up. You can gain insight into these reasons.

Picture yourself with that person. Imagine saying the things that are in your heart to that person.

Why We Don't Speak Up

Now, *imagine that person giving you the **worst possible response** to you telling your feelings.* Perhaps that response is that they say 'no' to you. Perhaps they reject you or mock you. Whatever your worst fear is, be clear in your mind. Write it down. Describe it. Face it.

This part is very important. You are silent for some good reason. You need to picture the worst possible response so you can work through your fear of speaking up. This stage helps you to discover just what it is that you are frightened of. Since most non-assertive people don't go any further than to feel frightened about speaking up, they often don't get to this point in the process.

If you do not assert yourself out of the fear of not being obeyed, of being powerless, then your anger is a way of keeping yourself from confronting that core insecurity of powerlessness. It will be essential that you spend a good deal of time studying your own thoughts and reactions to feeling powerless. The key is to accept it as a possibility, as something that might well happen. How can you cope with that powerlessness, if you refuse to coerce and force the other person into compliance? How can you cope and still say 'no!' to anger?

For the person who has been controlled by anger then, the provocative response that keeps you from asserting yourself may have to do with the other person saying "no!"

It could be that, or many other things. In any case, describe in detail how you see the worst possible response. Now that you have a frightening or provocative response in mind, you figure out what you can say to that person. What could you do to cope with the worst possible reaction? How would you adjust? What could you do to bounce back? By figuring out how to cope with the *worst* reaction, you will feel more capable and self-confident.

Think about what you really want, and create a vision of that as being something that helps everyone concerned. How would your vision spread benefit to people all around? How would it be a blessing? What about your vision energizes you? What would others have to see for it to energize them.

In this matter of <u>speaking from your heart</u>, the goal you have must be one that is positive, inspiring, and beneficial. You have to see, hear, taste, touch, and smell those benefits. They have to be real to you before you can help them become real to others. There must be enthusiasm in you before you can create interest in others.

Now after all of that, you need to recognize that the other person can still say 'no' to your dream. How can you cope with that?

Cope with Integrity

Imagine or create a way to cope that allows the other person their own freedom. After all, you want freedom, don't you? Find a way to handle the worst possible scenario that would leave you feeling proud of yourself, confident you really have done the right thing. If you really think you <u>must</u> have your way, you need to reflect on what the core fear is behind not having your own way. What is so awful if people don't do just as you want them to? Why is that so bad? Be rather blunt and brave with yourself. Face that fear.

Sometime this coping is simply to take a deep breath and relax yourself. Sometimes it is to admit, "You have a right to refuse, and there is really nothing I can do about that." Sometimes it would be to ask that other person for a helpful suggestion. You will want to imagine and rehearse responses that are respectful of the other person.

Before actually speaking up, you need practice. Perhaps you could practice being more assertive, at least in your mind. After all, it is not easy to give up anger but still have a reasonable impact. Practice the following format, writing out in your journal some possible dialogs. Be ready for the other person to do the very thing you fear. Try these ideas. Write them out in your journal, say them to yourself, and then see if you can use them in the actual situation.

1. **Agree** with the other person as far as you can. Most people defend themselves when someone says something irritating or critical. Instead of doing that, try to see the grain of truth in what they say. If you are beginning the conversation, stop and think of what you feel good about in relation to that person. If you can't seem to find something you respect, perhaps you shouldn't be talking to that person, since the danger is there of being overly critical.

2. **Tell what you have noticed** in the past: "I have seen this and that happen . . ." Here you will want to be quite specific. Tell what you saw. Tell what you heard. It is as if you are describing a videotape to a person who cannot see or hear the scene.

3 **Tell what you want**: "Instead of that, I would like us to do this . . ." Describe this again in video terms. This may be hard work, since we often want to say general things, like "You should be more respectful to me." That is too vague; tell what 'respectful' would look like. Tell what it would sound like. What would you see on a video if 'respect' were present?

4. **Benefits**: Mention how that would help, include your emotions: "If that happened, we will make more money, achieve more cooperation, etc., I would feel much more peaceful and comfortable . . ."

5. **Ask** for feedback: "What did you understand me to say? What

do you think about that? How do you feel?" Spend time listening attentively to the other person.

My Friend the Diary

Write down these dialogs. Then run through them regularly, talking out loud about what you want and how it would help if you could have that thing. Spend some time writing and some time reading what you have written out loud. This should make it much easier for you to assert yourself and speak up for what is important to you.

We want to be clear that assertiveness does not mean that every person will always do exactly what we want them to do. Sometimes people will deny our request. Sometimes that can be quite a setback. It makes us feel that it wasn't worth it to speak up. Watch out! That is just Anger trying to get back into control of your life. You can't always get what you want, but you can be more open and honest about what you want. Speak up. Be honest. Leave it with the other person. Then notice how it helps your own feelings to speak up, *even if others don't do what you want them to do*. Just speaking up helps us be more at peace.

To you who are reading this book to cope with angry people, there is a nice parallel here too. You need to speak up, just as the angry person needs that. Our angry friends need to learn more positive communication, and the ability to speak with desire but not with anger. They need to learn to accept the possibility that they won't get what they want.

You also need to learn to discover within yourself inspiring visions of the possible futures. You need to learn to speak of those visions with energy and enthusiasm. Your foe is not anger, I hope, but it is an emotion. It is fear. Only by taming the fear dragon in yourself will you be able to speak with truth and integrity.

If you talk to angry people with anger, you are simply making their delusion real. You are contributing to the madness, since your own anger 'proves' (in the insane logic of anger) that their original anger was justified.

Instead, focus on speaking about positive futures and inspiring goals. Say what you want. Speak from your heart. And then let if go. It is not your calling in life to control what other people do. When you speak about what you really want they may or may not pay much attention. That is not your concern. Your calling is to live a life of integrity and compassion.

If they care, they will work with you. If they don't then they need an extra dose of your compassion, since when we fail to care about others, we actually harm ourselves. We are all part of the network of life, and all things we do return to us. As a valued mentor once told me (likely quoting a poet he admired!):

"Unbeing returns upon one's unself,
Space being curved."

– Dr. Robert Finley

Chapter Ten

The Judo Technique with Angry People

If you have to deal with angry people who are not dangerous (that is, the truly dangerous bully who is both calm and brutal), but who is angry out of insecurity, this chapter may be of help. A skill most people need to develop is in this chapter, so no matter which side of the interaction you are on, this may help you. This chapter helps you develop a way to cope with someone who is chronically critical and negative. This would be someone you do not wish to leave, but a person you have trouble being around.

Note that if the angry person is truly a cold-blooded bully, there is no technique I know of to help you relate. Your only hope is to escape.

Sometimes I do a demonstration where one person pushes against me. I hold my hand up and invite the other person to resist me as I try to push them. They do resist, and if we are of the same strength, there is an impasse. No one is going anywhere. I then suggest that the other person continue to push against me – 'resist' if you will – and this time I quickly pull back. Just like in the sport of judo, this quick giving way puts the other person off balance and ends the contest.

Have I won or lost? The question is the wrong one. I have ended the impasse, and all I had to do was to move my hand quickly in the direction my opponent was pushing. Perhaps by exiting the impasse, I have helped both of us to win.

I studied at the Mental Research Institute in Palo Alto for a time, and learned about an experiment they once did. They brought two psychiatrists together, and told each man that he was going to meet a patient with the delusion that he was a psychiatrist. The two men began to compete to see who would be the doctor and who would be the patient. Suddenly the impasse was ended when one doctor said, "Well there are some things I have wanted to talk to someone about." He then described some dilemmas in his life, asking for advice on them. Obviously, this psychiatrist was the better therapist because he was flexible. He ended the impasse.

The one-down or "judo" technique is a method of dealing with angry, accusatory, or guilt-provoking people. This is a very difficult position to take, hard work! It violates almost every instinct about dealing with anger. It doesn't *always* work (what does?). However, when it does work, it works very well. In this position, the patient agrees to listen to the partner's accusations and try to find <u>some</u> truth in them, and agree with them, *without agreeing to change*!. The skills are:

Listen & reflect, emphasize "You are really angry **with me** over (repeat the issues)."

Self-disclose: "When you are that angry/critical, I feel frightened / ashamed / insecure."

Agree & extend: Look for a grain of truth in the accusation and agree. "I hate to admit it, but you have hit on a real weakness in me." "I do agree with you, and I sometimes think it may even be worse.

For example, (give details)" **Do not** make any offers to change, based on the anger; rather just take the position the partner's anger is justified, but you are not able to promise any great change, and may at times even get worse.

The notion here is that if I change in response to anger, I reinforce the anger. "I see you are angry and I will do *anything* so you won't be angry." Change because of anger? Now you have reinforced that anger! You train the other person to be angry to get his/her way.

BUT: Many people think they have to fight against the criticism and anger from others. There is a paradox here, too. If I fight and resist the anger, I am likely to be angry too. That means I reinforce the other person's anger, by saying in essence, "Your anger is a justifiable response, since I myself enjoy using it."

So the third way, agreeing there is an element of truth to what the other person says, but not changing because of the anger. Rather, one should change because of some better reasons, namely, because it is right, or because you and I negotiate something which is to my advantage. So it is a gentle but firm response. You are saying you understand the anger but you will not change because of it. You do not reinforce it by fighting against the anger; you do not reinforce it by giving in.

Why we should do this - Value systems

I have had some success with this technique with Christian patients, pointing out that Jesus told us to go two miles when we are expected to go one. The context for that was the Roman soldiers had the right to compel any citizen to carry their packs, but only for a single mile. If a Christian carried the pack for an extra mile, that would be an extraordinary event. It would get the attention of the soldier whose pack they were carrying. It would possibly create a positive reverberation in society. That soldier would be kinder to the next person, and the next person might be kinder in turn. Jesus' commandment to go the second mile is true genius.

Similarly, Christians are obligated to do <u>more</u> agreeing with criticism than the other person has a right to expect. Note that Jesus didn't say you need to enjoy carrying the pack, or even that you must be sincere about carrying it. You are quite free to resent it and dislike doing it. You are simply obligated to do it.

Some people reject the Bible. That is all right. Another analogy for this is the Japanese self-defense art of Aikido, in which one cooperates with the attacker in a surprising or unusual way, and thus nullifies the attack. Like Judo, where the master uses the attacker's own strength to defeat him, aikido relies on the strength of the attack to counter it. My own aikido teacher used to claim that if you try to fight with a true aikido master, you end up being friends at the end of the fight. Some "new age" folks who don't relate to Jesus may relate to the aikido notion. Aikido was developed in a Buddhist environment. Buddhism emphasizes compassion and cooperation. Emphasize the wisdom of Buddha. He taught that suffering was the result of inappropriate desires. Being defensive would not be what Buddha would teach. He would suggest you follow the aikido path.

But it is Counter-Intuitive

This approach completely contradicts our instinctive methods of handling accusations, criticism, and anger. You may want to bear in mind that our instinctive methods are arising our of our instinct-driven *reptile brain*. Throughout our history as a species, the reptile brain's three stress responses (flight, fight, or freeze) worked well. But in society you aren't going to be eaten, and you aren't going to kill and eat the critical person. So we have to question our instincts.

Specifically, our instincts tell us to NEVER do step Two, admit the vulnerability that anger and criticism creates in us. Our defensiveness is like running or fighting the aggressor. At a core level, we actually unconsciously believe we will be killed and eaten. But our instincts are mistaken. When your wife or husband or boss criticizes, it is unlikely to go beyond verbal criticism. Try this and see.

Chapter Eleven

Criticism: Does It Really Help?
Handling your desire to criticize another person

> "Sometimes a man has to rise above principle."
> – Senator Everett Dirkson, R, Ill. (1896-19690

I have come to think that criticism is another symptom of anger. If you are noticing that you do a good deal of criticizing, this chapter may give you some challenging food for thought. Let's start with a definition:

Criticism: *censure, condemnation, disapproval, or reproach*. When you criticize someone, you are condemning or disapproving of them. Naturally, they are less than happy about that as a general rule, and will try to *defend* themselves, a perfectly understandable reaction.

I'd like to talk to you a bit about criticism since I find that seems to always be present with anger problems. Since we talked earlier about compassion, I thought some discussion about criticism would make a nice counterpoint.

This is a very hard habit. After all, we all have desires, wishes that the world would be different. And just often enough, when we criticize, people listen and make some changes. This rewards that critical eye, the blaming and critical voice. We criticize more and more.

Then one day, people stop doing what we had wanted them to do. They go back to the old habits. What has happened?

The Flaw in Criticism

Criticism implies that you are in a superior position to the person being criticized. People have a tendency to resent anything that makes them feel as if they are losing freedom. This is known as *reactance* and seems to be built into all human beings. Criticism implies that by suggesting that you are the authority over that other person. That causes them to react emotionally and negatively.

So criticism is a very dangerous activity in relationships, since it leads to defensiveness, which leads to more criticism on your part. It is like you are saying, "They just aren't getting it, I'll say it some more." The more your criticize, the more they defend or attack you, and the situation deteriorates.

Criticism – if it were a person – would promise you that if people will just hear and respond to your criticism, you will really be happy. Criticism makes us feel self-righteous. We are convinced that we are right. So it is only logical that criticism will help. I suggest it does not. Criticism simply degrades relationships and feelings.

If you doubt this, review in your own mind when other people criticized you. How did it work? Were you glad or perhaps defensive and angry? Review your times of criticizing others. Where they thrilled to get your input, or perhaps angry and defensive? What about when you criticize yourself? Do you feel empowered and enthusiastic, or defective and depressed? Criticism is counter-factual *and not a helpful way to talk to yourself.*

Generally, people are too critical of themselves. There are some people who probably aren't critical enough, but most of us are not like that. Criticism is vastly over-rated as a way of helping ourselves to improve.

Steps toward productive criticism

Try to get over it by yourself

See if you can overcome your own tendency to criticize. After all, your first job in a relationship is to *enjoy* the other person. If you are thinking critical thoughts, you cannot enjoy that person. You can enjoy that person more if you can find something positive about the problem situation. Sit down by yourself with a sheet of paper and do this exercise:

(A)   Recognize the problem is not the other person, it is your own critical thoughts.

(B)   Describe the situation that you object to. This may be difficult because you might notice as you try to describe the *situation* you also throw in your own judgements. Try to keep it a description of behaviors, things you can see and hear.

(C)   Describe your own *judgement* about the situation. Again, it is your judgement, not the situation itself that can be changed.

(D)   Now try to discover something *positive* about the problem. Look for some way you might be benefitting from the very problem you object to. Look for a more *compassionate* or understanding way of understanding the situation.

EXAMPLE: My husband or wife is cool and distant and irritable with me.

(A) *It's my problem, with my own thinking:* My partner is who he is, and my irritation is really my own criticism of him. Maybe he (she) is only cool and distant at times, not always, and my own thinking makes me miss those times.

(B) *The situation:* He looks away when I talk to him, and seldom hugs or touches me.

(C) *My current thoughts:* I do so much for him, I am loyal to him, but he won't show warmth to me.

(D) *How is this actually a positive?* Why not look at it just as the way he was raised, with more reserve and distance. And it can help me to learn to be less dependent on how people treat me; I can learn to be happy and cheerful without having the crutch of someone else supporting me emotionally. I can treat him with warmth whether he is warm back or not. I can notice times he is more warm. I can change myself instead of trying to change him. Why not look at it as a sign that my partner is having a hard time and needs more understanding and compassion from me? Why not look at it as a chance to give warmth and love in a non-demanding way, in which I don't do it to get something but only to be helpful to the other person?

The right way, the mature way, is to recognize a great truth, namely that your criticism is simply based on your own notions, beliefs, and prejudices. Everyone has such ideas, and they are all different. The fact is that when you criticize someone, you are likely to be listening too much to the idea that you are right about something. "My way is right" cries the critical voice.

But opinions aren't so much a question of right or wrong as they are a question of helpful or useful. Helpful opinions produce useful outcomes, like respect, teamwork, cooperation, and even love. Unhelpful opinions produce the opposite. So try to rise above the idea of true or not true, and look more broadly. Is it helpful or unhelpful?

Does Criticism Ever Help?

What do we do about being critical of others? Your best and highest option is to simply get over it yourself. Drop the thought of criticizing. Ask yourself sincerely and truthfully whether it will make a difference in a year, or a month, or even a week. Even if your criticism would be helpful a week from now, it is probably not your job to offer that criticism. If you are not in a position of being responsible for the output of the other person (if you are not their boss at work, in other words), then you simply have no place in criticizing.

Even if you are a boss, you probably ought to recall that Bass and Avolio, in their studies on leadership, found conclusively that bosses who relied on criticizing past performance has the worst impact on workplace productivity. Such bosses are actually worse than no boss at all, since they degrade the performance of those they "supervise." Obviously, I used the scare quotes around supervise because I don't consider that real supervision.

As for the best leaders, Lao Tzu taught, the people say, "We did it ourselves." Great leaders make people believe they are doing things themselves. The great leaders bring people's strengths together while making their weaknesses irrelevant.

"What if I can't be calm about this?"

If you can't get over it by yourself: Here is an idea that may help you: We really have no right to criticize each other without permission. When you criticize someone, you are acting as if you are superior to them. All people have a right to dignity and to criticize someone without their permission robs them of dignity.

(A) Ask permission to criticize: "I have a problem I need your help with. It involves something you are doing. May I talk to you about it?" If that person won't give you permission, you have to do a great deal of fence-mending or strengthening of the relationship so it will be more natural for the person to accept your complaint.

You should also ask the person to hear you out completely before he or she says anything about your complaint. Ask him to give you time to completely explain your position. Asking it this way shows real respect and consideration for the other person.

(B) State the criticism in "video description" language: What would you see on a videotape showing the problem happening. Stick to what you can see and hear; don't talk about your judgement or opinions about the problem, just the problem itself.

(C) Tell what that videotape would look like *if the problem were gone*. What would you see instead? What would be present? How would that help you? Too often, criticism simply emphasizes a kind of 'get rid of' attitude. That isn't helpful. You need to speak from your heart. You need to have a positive vision. If all you want to do is get rid of something, you don't have that positive vision, and you can't really expect anything good to come from your criticism.

(D)   *Release the problem:* "I realize I cannot force you to do this, it is something that I would like but it may not be something you are willing to do."

(E)   *Listen:* Find out what the person thinks about your request. Do not interrupt, especially if it sounds like the person didn't understand. Just listen, and keep listening until the other person is through talking.

As this discussion proceeds, put your energy into *taking turns talking.* Ask the other person not to interrupt you, and do not interrupt the other person. Be patient and listen carefully until the other person is through talking. Polite fights are more productive than rude ones in which each interrupts the other.

Even if the other person interrupts you, you are not justified in interrupting him or her. Manners are most important here, and the other person not having good manners doesn't mean you should join in rudeness.

Watch the Watch!

Some people find that actually *timing* the conversation helps. That is, each person talks for a specific amount of time (usually seven minutes) while the other just listens; then the other person talks while the first person listens. *Allowing the other person dignity is vital, especially when the other person has bad habits of communication and doesn't seem to "deserve" good treatment.*

Another version of this "timed argument" is the One Minute Drill. Here one person - person A - talks for a minute, plus or minus a half a minute or so. The second person - person B - tries to summarize what the message is, and asks for a rating on how accurate B is at understanding A. If the rating is around 90% or better, then B talks, and A listens. After a minute, A summarizes B's message and asks for a rating. Again, the rating needs to get to 90% in B's eyes before A has the floor again. In any case, taking turns is a key skill.

"But what if the other person *never* gets through talking, they just go on and on?"

The best response to that is to spend hours, if necessary, just listening, and not trying to change that person. Their continuing to talk means something, but we don't know what it means until we listen for a long time. So practice good listening skills. You might consider that this is an opportunity to learn to be a much better listener than you ordinarily would be. You might ask the person why they continue to repeat themselves, what they are expecting? But basically, a person who continues on and on is a person who has probably never really been heard, and if you can hear him, you can heal him.

In summary: Criticism is a very dangerous activity, and should be avoided if possible; if you have to criticize, make sure you are doing it in a relationship of respect and warmth, make sure you follow a pattern of respecting the other person and allowing that other person his dignity. Follow this rule: Always ask permission to criticize; if you don't have permission, you shouldn't go ahead with the criticism. You have to get over it by yourself. Find a way to cope, reframe it as a positive opportunity to learn and grow, treat yourself to some special experience . . . but don't criticize without permission.

How can we deal with criticism when it is aimed at us? In Chapter Ten, we focused on the Judo response. Let's take that a bit further.

In Tibetan Buddhism the purpose of life is to perfect one's character. This is a challenging task, of course. Often we are blind to our own flaws and shortcomings. The Buddhist teachers point out that our enemies always attack us on our weakest point. Since our goal should be to master that weakness, we really should be very grateful for the attack. It teaches us where we are weak. "Your worst enemy," say the Buddhist teachers, "is actually your best friend. Only the enemy will show you your weakness."

So if you can find it in your heart, try to be grateful. It may be there are some "deal breakers" that you are engaging in. Suppose you are married, and the criticism is over excessive spending, an affair with another person, drug use, viewing pornography, violence or verbal abuse. In this case, you must take the criticism to heart and begin to work through your resistence to change. Otherwise, your marriage may well be over.

Similarly, a boss who confronts you with what is unacceptable behavior, failure to perform, is someone who must be listened to. Such things we can call "deal breakers," or conditions that end your marriage or your employment.

Nevertheless, I do not think it is typically wise to

immediately try to change. Most criticism is not really over deal breakers, but rather over preferences. The critical person is trying to change you by intimidating you with anger. He or she may not realize that is the intention, but it is. Hurry and change??? Remember, you might be rewarding the anger.

You can say, with sincerity, "Your point is a good one. Perhaps you are more right than you can imagine. That is a weakness. In fact, the longer I live, the more I notice it. I have to warn you that you will probably have to cope with that weakness for some time to come. It might get worse, and I would advise you to mentally prepare yourself for that."

I actually have some very mixed feelings about the notion of resolving our weaknesses. It sounds like a good thing, and I am sure I should be in favor of it. But frankly, there is very little evidence that it is of much value. Marcus Buckingham and Donald Clifton's book, <u>Now, Discover Your Strengths</u> presents us with some very good data from the Gallup organization. Based on polling of many thousands of businesses, workers, and supervisors, they found that the idea of improving weaknesses seemed to be a dead end.

The opposite tack, building on strengths, seems to work much better. Buckingham and Clifton learned that businesses spent millions of dollars trying to fix weaknesses in their employees, and there is almost no return on that investment. It is wasted resource, both in terms of money and in terms of the energy the employees put into the efforts.

Instead, they found that discovering the employee strengths and building on those what a more successful approach. All groups, whether it is a workplace or a family, are composed of people with very different gifts and talents. People are best when they discover their talents and grow them. They contribute the most to the group when their contribution is unique.

Yes, there are "deal breaker" behaviors that must be changed if the relationship is to survive. But most of the criticisms I hear people say about each other are more in the category of simple differences in opinion. If I order salmon at the restaurant, can you justifiably say I must change and order steak? No, my tastes are my own, as are yours, and I respect yours. I hope you will respect mine. Most things people want each other to change are simply differences in taste. Instead of trying to change each other, let's rejoice in our diversity.

Like the parable of "Stone Soup" when we cast our diverse gifts into the common pot, the result is a rich and nourishing broth. If every person casts in a turnip, all we have is a vegetable broth that, when cooked, is only suitable for serving to the damned souls in hell.

So rejoice in your unique gifts, and don't be hasty to change yourself into something that is a pale imitation of who you really are, obscuring your own *talents so that others can wander aimlessly in their own mind-numb complacency. Be yourself, and rejoice in the person that you are.*

Finally, let me ask for a favor. Please don't email me and tell me you like cooked turnips.

Chapter Twelve

Activate Your Frontal Lobes:
One Minute to Increased Intelligence and Creativity

L et's cut to the chase here: When you are calm and experiencing positive emotions, you are more intelligent. You know this by now. You know, do you not, that you have done something while either scared or angry that later seemed dumb?

Of course you have. So have I. Sometimes we wonder, "What was I thinking?" Now you know. You were thinking with your alligator brain. Don't hold that against yourself. Everyone thinks with their alligator brain at times. Be compassionate. It is part of your natural heritage.

In this chapter you will learn a simple way to shift energy back to your **prefrontal cortex**, the most integrative and insightful part of your brain. It is a simple, three step process I call Shifting Up.

To Shift Up to prefrontal cortex energy, you have to *recognize* that you are under stress. You are upset, running scared, or indignant. Maybe disgusted and withdrawing. Any strong negative emotion shifts down the cortex and slides you down into alligator thinking. This is generally a case of some person threatening or irritating us, but not always. Sometimes it is just our own imagination, worry about problems that haven't happened ("Oh no, what if THIS happened?").

As soon as you recognize you are under stress, move into Shift Up mode. Three steps: Shift, Recall, and Ask. One, Two, Three. Simple, easy to practice.

Shift Up: A One Minute Exercise

1. **SHIFT** attention away from the brain (self talk, fears, and so on) and down to your breathing and heart. Just breathe in slowly and feel your heart beating. *Notice carefully how your heart feels. Notice how your breathing affects the heart rate, and how your heart affects your breathing.* Do this for about thirty seconds. Keep your full attention on the region of the heart. (This calming process interrupts the anger or fear.)

2. **RECALL** and relive a positive emotion, one where you felt peaceful, confident, and secure. Think of a time when you felt genuine love for someone. Keep your focus on that feeling. *Fill the heart with that emotion. Let the memory of that feeling activate your frontal lobes.* Do this for about thirty seconds. (The energy begins to move into the prefrontal cortex.)

3. **ASK** yourself, "What is the highest and best way to handle this situation?" Listen carefully to your heart. Listen for a thought from your frontal lobes, the high-speed center for creativity and integration of advanced insights. Listen for a change of feeling in your heart. Tune in to your heart. Trust what comes and do it!

Repetition and Mastery

I have found that you work on a particular topic, such as your anger at a person or situation. Set aside some time, and take note of how much your are upset about the issue. Scale your upset feeling from 1 - 10, with 1 = I am completely at peace, and 10 = I am so agitated I cannot stand it.

Now you have that scaling, do a Shift Up process on that topic.

1. Shift your attention to your breathing and heart. Keep the focus there for 20 - 30 seconds.

2. Recall the feelings of a very good time; feelings like love, confidence, or happiness.

3. Ask yourself an inspiring and enlightening question about the topic. "What is the highest and best way for me to see that situation?" is an example.

Notice what changes you sense. Think about the topic again. What rating do you give it now? Are you lower? Most people will be at this point.

If you are lower, but not at a 'one' rating, repeat the process. Keep repeating the Shift Up process until you come to a place where you really are at a 'one.' That may take some time. But it will come.

The more you practice this in minor issues (or even when you feel neutral) the easier it becomes. There are two switches in your brain (the 'amygdalas' that we have discussed earlier, located on both sides of your brain) that need to be reprogrammed and it takes a lot of practice. As you know by now, the amygdala takes a long time to reprogram. Longer periods of nurturing and expanding positive feelings are great investments. The more you enjoy positive feelings, the more you __can__ enjoy positive feelings.

Questions & Answers: Notes on the Shift Up process

"When I try to Shift, my mind just keeps going on the stress."

Occasionally people have trouble with the Shift phase. Their mind is too active, too much going on. It may help you to think about the difference between *thinking* and *sensing*. In the Shift Up process, we change our experience from thinking (active mind, self-talk) to sensing (quiet mind, waiting and noticing without inner commentary).

When we begin to sense something, our attention is on our senses - our feelings, our internal experiences. There is no attempt to control or influence the breath or the heartbeat. It is a simple and quiet observing. It may seem almost like a psychological quiet descending on the mind. As we sense, our thinking quiets downs.

Imagine a cat watching a mouse sticking its head around a corner. The cat is quiet, focused, attention totally on sight and hearing. That's somewhat like this sensing of the heart. There is a quite sensing of the inner experience, the effortless rhythm of breathing, the reassuring beating of the heart. These inner experiences have traditionally been used to teach people about meditation. Instead of meditating on your heartbeat or on your breathing for twenty minutes, I encourage you to simply focus on the heartbeat for a half minute or so.

It is also possible that you would benefit from a more extensive mental training that Shift Up can provide. For example, use Autogenic Training every day for twenty minutes. That exercise is found in Appendix I.

"It bugs me to think about my breathing. How will that help?"

A few people become frightened when they focus on their breathing or on their heart. They seem to have a deep distrust of inner processes, and they scrutinize their own breathing as if it were a problem. People with this habit will sometimes actually find their breathing speeding up or their heart racing when they practice this. In that case, there is some desensitization that needs to be done. The anxious person needs to learn to relax while focusing on breathing.

Here is a simple exercise that will generally help. I have written a bit more about this in Appendix II. You are going to breathe attentively for about ten minutes, twice a day. As you do this for longer times, you will naturally feel less anxious and eventually focus on breath will relax you.

First, focus your attention on your inner experience. Notice any tension that might be present in your body. Don't try to change anything about that. Just notice it.

Next, count while you breathe in. Count to three. Hold your breath for a moment or two, and then slowly breathe out. Count while you breathe out. Try to count to about nine or twelve as you breathe out. Pause for a couple of moments. Now breathe in again to the count of three. Pause, breathe out to the count of twelve. Pause. And continue this. After ten minutes, notice how you feel. Notice how your body feels. Is there any tension or anxiety? Is there any anger or resentment? Probably you will notice that negative emotions are gone. If you have done a good job of counting, your mind was unable to think about the kinds of things that would maintain a negative emotional state.

If thoughts intrude into this exercise, just simply return to the exercise. Quietly say, "That is just thinking, thinking." Return to the counting.

"What kinds of positive feeling should I practice?"

Some psychologists now believe there are three core positive feelings: compassion (a feeling of understanding of others, together with a desire to be of help), curiosity, and delight or joy. Love, the magical combination of all three, is great. Times when curiosity was predominant, or when compassion moved you to help others are also worthy of practice. Actually, any good positive emotion seems to stimulate positive thought, creativity, insight, and peace.

Research into emotions supports this concept. There are very specific outcomes to the negative emotions. Anger = fight; fear = flight, and despair = freeze. There is a very specific relationship between the negative feeling and the behavior.

The same is not at all true of positive emotions. Professor Barbara Fredrickson has found that positive emotions broaden our options. They make us more flexible. They make it easier for us to learn, to grow, and to create.

Take the example of creativity. We can always use more creativity, more inventions. But there is not one single emotion that creates creativity. People can be creative out of love, out of hope, out of excitement, out of intellectual curiosity.

So it is with all positive behaviors. Any positive emotion can promote a wide variety of positive behaviors. So it is not necessary to practice any specific positive emotion. Any positive feeling will give you some useful leverage.

Teresa Amabile is professor of management at Harvard University. She has studied creativity for many years, and now can clearly show that positive emotions are the stimulus to the best creativity. She found that positive emotions would "prime" the brain to invent and create. In daily diaries, the managers and staff in several large companies described their activities. She found that the day after a particularly pleasing day, the workers were much more likely to invent or create a solution to a tough problem.

So when the going gets tough, the smart may tell a joke, or go shopping, or watch a funny movie. The smart do something to get their frontal lobes engaged.

That's why I encourage you to make a habit of shifting your emotions from moderate or low into a higher level, a level of happiness, zest, enthusiasm, and gratitude. I want you to be happier.

"What am I supposed to be feeling? What is supposed to change?"

I am asked what sorts of changes to look for when asking oneself for the highest and best way to deal with a problem. I find there are several areas of change, and some people find one and some another.

– FEELING: A change of emotional reaction about the situation. When it occurs, you notice a shift away from the 'alarm' feeling to a more peaceful or accepting feeling.

– PERSPECTIVE: Things literally look different. If you could look back on a situation ten years from now, it certainly looks different does it not? Less intense? Less important? We see this happen quickly when people begin to practice the Shift Up process. This may be part of the creative process that Teresa Amabile studies.

– INTENTION: Often people begin to re-evaluate their own goals, finding that what seemed important to do now seems unimportant. Other goals take their place. Our wants and desires change, and naturally our feelings also change. This is another aspect of intelligence and creativity. We see things anew.

Where is the Answer?

The key here is that wisdom comes from inside of yourself. There is an old Sufi (a Persian mystical sect) story about that. It seems that Nasrudin, a "foolish' spiritual teacher (a teacher who plays the role of a jester or clown), was seen madly riding his donkey from one side of town to the other, as if searching for something. Finally the people in the town stopped him and asked, "Mullah Nasrudin, what are you looking for?"

"My donkey!" was the frantic reply.

Like the absent minded professor who searches his desk frantically for the glasses perched on his own head, we look outside ourselves for answers we can find within. The answers may not come as we expect, but they do come. In fact, when the answer / response from within is not what our brain is expecting is exactly the time when we see the most insight and creativity. Experience with this process convinces me that within each of us is a great deal of untapped wisdom.

Using the Whole Brain

You have heard that we only use 10% of our brain's potential. There may be some truth to this old idea. We certainly are able to gain access to wisdom and peace by the Shift Up process. Try to practice it throughout the day, make it a habit, and look to your heart's wisdom to solve your daily problems.

Assignment: Put a band-aid on a finger, or switch your watch to the opposite wrist, or tie a string around your finger. Every time you notice that change, take one minute, shift up, ask an intelligent question about how you can <u>right now</u> handle something with more understanding, more insight, more creativity.

Write down the results of shifting up. Track that in your diary. Believe me when I tell you that the more you practice, the more you will succeed.

When you are on the receiving end of anger, try to implement the Shift Up process. This is a key technique, and I believe it will help almost anyone. Give it a try for a week, try it ten times a day, and I believe you may end up keeping it for a lifetime.

Sometimes people give themselves criticism for not practicing at the time they need it. Well, your heart is in the right place, but I don't think self-criticism is the way to get you to use the Shift Up skill. Instead, you might want to practice it <u>after</u> you 'should have.' That is simple. Just do it later, and don't punish yourself for not doing it at the time. Your use will get more and more timely.

Chapter Thirteen

Other Voices

It is not the critic who counts, not the man who points out how the strong man stumbled, or where the doer of deeds could have done them better. The credit belongs to the man who is actually in the arena; whose face is marred by dust and sweat and blood; who strives valiantly, who errs and comes short again and again; who knows the great enthusiasms, the great devotions, and spends himself in a worthy cause; who, at the best, knows in the end the triumph of high achievement; and who at the worst, at least fails while daring greatly, so that his place shall never be with those cold and timid souls who know neither victory nor defeat.
　　　– Teddy Roosevelt

Who else is working on anger? Not as many people as I would hope, but there are some good people out there. Here I will mention a few of them. You may want to read their thoughts also.

Steven Stosey has a system of transforming anger based on compassion. His book is called "You Don't Have to Take It Anymore."

Thich Nhat Hanh is a Buddhist teacher. His book is called "Anger: Wisdom for Cooling the Flames."

Dr. Raymond DiGiuseppe, is professor of psychology, St. John's University in New York City. He has made some excellent points on anger and problems it causes. He said, "Anger management? I hate the term. It implies we can keep anger under wraps. It doesn't imply treatment or therapy for a problem."

Can we live without anger? It does appear possible. In the book, *Destructive Emotions* by Daniel Goleman and His Holiness the Dalai Lama, we learn of experienced meditators who have so trained their brains that they do not react with anger to any provocation. By years of diligent effort, they have shaped themselves to be joyful and cheerful, resilient and intelligent in all situations. Richard Davidson, professor at the University of Wisconsin, has done brain scans of Buddhist monks that show them as some of the happiest people on the planet, with astonishingly high levels of energy in the "happiness centers" of the brain (the left prefrontal regions).

Do you have to move to India and meditate in a cave for twenty years to achieve this? Well, maybe . . . but that is a silly option. Rather, let's learn the real lesson. Davidson and other brain scientists have clearly shown that we literally shape our brain by our behavior. The Buddhist monks are simply good examples to all of us. We do not need to move to India, but we can seek the same things they seek, loving kindness and inner strength. When we practice compassion and patience, those centers are strengthened in our brain. It literally grows. By the same token, those who become upset and enraged are also shaping their brains, weakening the frontal lobes and strengthening the monkey and reptile complexes.

People who practice the skill of forgiveness, for example, certainly raise their happiness levels. Things don't bother them as much, they bounce back more quickly from negative events. Because they are not ruminating on injustices and old injuries, they are more intelligent and insightful. They are better at creativity. They are naturally more able to influence other people. Appendix I has Autogenic Training, and Appendix II has instructions on breathing exercises. These are the sorts of skills that you can practice to improve your own brain functioning.

So I invite you to apply what we have shared in this book. Renounce hate, anger and fighting, and embrace love, peace, and brotherhood. Practice forgiveness each day. It is the right thing do. We have no right to coerce another being do anything. Only by kindness, by love and patience can we influence truly and rightfully. Only when we love another so much than we have no need for them to be different will they change. Every other way will eventually fail.

You are embarking on the greatest adventure in the universe, the conquest of your own self. Ralph Waldo Emerson said, "What lies behind us and what lies before us are small matters compared to what lies within us."

What lies within you is love. It is the greatest force in the universe. With it you can do anything; without it you will never do anything of value, though the world worships you. Your possessions will vanish, and your works will crumble and disappear. Your name will be forgotten. All turns to dust.

But your love will live forever.

"The most difficult things for people to do apparently is not feel resentful when someone does a mean thing to them. Remember this, that no outward thing can hurt you inside. Oh we're more than this garment of clay which we wear. That which activates the garment of clay is the important thing. And no outward thing can hurt that - but a wrong reaction to an outward thing can hurt that. You see, we hurt ourselves by our wrong actions or our wrong reactions. When we get rid of wrong actions and wrong reactions then we will never more be hurt inside. Now if someone does a mean thing to you, so far he is only hurting himself. You're not hurt at all in the process, unless through a wrong reaction, you hurt yourself by a feeling of bitterness. Or perhaps you even feel anger and do a mean thing in return. Then you hurt yourself."

– Peace Pilgrim, Salt Lake City, Utah, 1955

Who was Peace Pilgrim?

Some people are curious about this quote with which I close the last chapter. Who is (or was) Peace Pilgram? This following paragraph is from the website:

http://www.peacepilgrim.net

From 1953 to 1981 a silver haired woman calling herself only "Peace Pilgrim" walked more than 25,000 miles on a personal pilgrimage for peace. She vowed to "remain a wanderer until mankind has learned the way of peace, walking until given shelter and fasting until given food." In the course of her 28 year pilgrimage she touched the hearts, minds, and lives of thousands of individuals all across North America. Her message was both simple and profound. It continues to inspire people all over the world:

"This is the way of peace:
     overcome evil with good,
     and falsehood with truth,
     and hatred with love."

May we all walk in the pathway of peace.
Lynn Johnson
http://drlynnjohnson.com

Appendix 1: Autogenic Training

The autogenic training exercises below can help you recover from anxiety, stress, and tension. These exercises have also been shown to aid in the recovery from certain diseases in which stress plays a part, such as headaches, high blood pressure, some stomach problems, and so on. People who practice some form of meditation every day are clearly healthier and age more slowly than those who don't. If you want to age quickly, pleased don't practice Autogenic Training, and especially do not practice it every day.

Autogenic training was developed by a German doctor, Johannes Schultz, as a way of bringing the benefits of meditation to westerners without the eastern mysticism. He recommended you start with one skill, such as heaviness in the limbs, and master that, before you move on to more advanced skills.

Repeat every phrase, silently, in your mind, <u>three times</u>. Say the phrase in a quiet, thoughtful way. Pause after and notice how you feel. Focus on your feelings for two or three breaths. Practice each set of exercises until you are quite comfortable with them.

Practice at least once, better twice a day. The more often you return your body to a state of restful quiet, the more energy and self-control you will experience.

Start by simply focusing on your breathing for about thirty seconds, or perhaps five to ten breaths. Just sense the feeling of air filling your lungs, the feeling of air leaving the lungs. Focus on sensing and let your mind naturally begin to quiet down. Then begin Set 1.

Set 1:

I feel quite quiet. . .   I am easily relaxed. . .

My right arm feels heavy and relaxed. . . My left arm feels heavy and relaxed. . . My arms feel heavy and relaxed . . .

My right leg feels heavy and relaxed. . . My left leg feels heavy and relaxed. . . My arms and legs feel heavy and relaxed. . My hips and stomach are quiet and relaxed . . . My shoulders are heavy and relaxed and relaxed . . My breathing is calm and regular . . . My face is smooth and quiet . . .I am beginning to feel quite relaxed. . .

Practice Set 1 until you can rapidly feel a sense of heaviness in the arms and legs. This may happen the first time you do this, or it may take some days. Just be patient and look for mastery.

Set 2:

My right hand is warm . . . My left hand is warm . . . Warmth flows into my hands . . . My hands are warm . . . My right foot is warm . . . My left foot is warm . . . My hands and feet are warm . . . Warmth flows into my hands and feet . . . My eyes are comfortably warm and peaceful . . . My forehead is cool and my eyes are warm . . . I am warm and peaceful . . .

This set of skills improves the circulation. When you feel a definite sense of warmth in the arms and legs, in the hands and feet, you know that the parasympathetic nervous system has opened up your arteries. Your blood pressure has come down nicely and you are increasing the DHEA - nature's recovery and growth hormone - in your system.

Set 3:

I am beginning to feel quite relaxed . . . My breathing is calm and regular. . . My heartbeat is calm and regular . . I am at peace. . . Sounds and sights around contribute to peace . . . Peace goes with me though out the day . . . There is nothing to bother and nothing to disturb . . .

Here you want to experience a peace and tranquility that comes from having a well-trained mind. A prepared mind is able to cope with all sorts of stresses without going into an alarm stage. Fear and anger only disrupt your thinking and don't contribute anything to actual problem solving.

Set 4:

Just for today, I will anger not . . . Just for today I will worry not . . . Today I will be grateful and humble . . . Today I will do my work with appreciation . . . Today, I will be kind to all . . .

Set 5: I enjoy the people in my life . . . I enjoy my life . . .I have good will for people . . . I feel patience and compassion toward all people . . . I feel peaceful and forgiving . . . I feel grateful . . .

At this point, picture in your mind various positive images about people you know. You might pick someone you are angry with, say, "I forgive you" to that person, and picture wonderful things happening to that person. Picture good things happening to those you love. Imagine yourself achieving things you feel proud about. Picture yourself healthy and happy.

If you wish to make your own phrases, use the principle that you are describing things as if they are already happening. Speak in positive terms, such as, "tobacco is unpleasant to me" rather than "I don't use tobacco." Generally, you would avoid negative words like "no, not, never, don't" and so on. Give yourself a positive goal. In set 4, we say, "I will anger not . . ." and then we embrace a positive goal, "I will be grateful and humble . . ." The mind likes to go *toward* something rather than away from something.

So if you want to view tobacco (or any bad habit) as a bad thing, be sure to follow up with a positive goal that you can move towards.

Special procedure: Patients sometimes want some relief from a troubling emotion such as jealousy or resentment, or from discomfort and pain. Try the following after some autogenic training. When your mind is quiet and peaceful, do these steps:

What RATING do you give your unpleasant feeling (including pain!)? See that number, and push it away from you. Watch it leave for about 30 seconds to one minute.

What COLOR is your emotion? Imagine that feeling or pain being located in a part of your body. Look to the edges. Where does the feeling end? Imagine your body can produce a natural bleach. See your body bleach out that color with a natural chemical the body can produce. Notice the edges of the feeling as they start to fade first.

Suppose the feeling were in a container, like a gallon jar or a quart container. What AMOUNT is your emotion? See a container with that amount, and open a small hole in the bottom and feel the liquid run out. Feel all aspects of it. Is it warm? Cool? Cold? Is it runny? Or thick? Is it sticky? Or slippery? Is the liquid oily? Or watery? Shake off your fingers and watch the liquid run down into a drain and away.

What SOUND would your emotion be? If it were a voice, what would it say? If it were music, what kind of music would it be? If it were some other sound, what would it be? Do something to reduce or turn off the sound, or change it in some positive way.

Return to what RATING you give your emotion, and continue. Rate the strength of the feeling now, and then push it away. Imagine the color, and bleach it out. Look at the amount, and feel it run out of a container. Listen to the sound and modify it. Repeat 2 to 6 times. Notice what difference it makes. Whenever your body needs this kind of break, it will signal you by giving you the pain or the emotion that you have just worked on. Each time, thank the body for the reminder. Spend some quiet time working with these techniques. Notice whether you feel refreshed and rested afterwards.

Whenever you feel particularly good, comfortable, or confident, notice that feeling and welcome it. Thank yourself for making that feeling happen. Remind yourself of these good times as often as possible. Good feelings are like music: the more you practice, the more skilled you become.

DEALING WITH IRRITANTS

Once I took my family camping. We went to a desert location famed for hiking and mountain biking trails. I had found a campground that was inexpensive, and arranged for a reservation to pitch the family tent.

My wife, I and my four children were soon snuggling down into our sleeping bags, the next day's planned adventures drifting happily through our thoughts.

I was just feeling sleepy when I heard a loud sound out on the road that ran past the campground. It was the sound of a truck using "jake brakes" as it headed down the hill into town. The driver shifted into a lower gear to help slow his vehicle. BAPPPPPPPP it rattled as it slowed for the descent. "That's pretty loud," I thought to myself. "I hope it is the last truck of the night.

Actually, it was the first.

I suppose truckers like to drive at night. They have less irritations and other drivers to cope with. They can deliver their produce and milk and bread in the middle of the night, so it is fresh for the next morning. We like things fresh.

I myself like fresh things. I just didn't know I was going to pay the price for it. The price seemed to be a sleepless night.

A few minutes later, another jake-braking truck started down that same hill. I thought, "No wonder this campground is so inexpensive!"

Around me was the rhythmic breathing of my family. A heart-warming sound, but one that tonight was causing me a pang of envy. I wished I were asleep as they obviously were. My wife seemed dead to the world in her cosy sleeping bag. I stared at the roof of the tent.

An idea came to me. I would try my Autogenic Training. I began with heaviness in the arms and legs. Then I focused on warmth in the hands and the feet. Soon I was relaxed. Not sleeping yet, but more relaxed.

Then I began to desensitize myself to the sound of the trucks and their engine brakes.

"The sounds of trucks reminds me to relax," I said.

"When I hear trucks, I remember to relax.

"Trucks remind me to relax."

"Trucks carry away muscle tension."

"When I hear trucks I feel relaxed and sleepy."

"The sound of trucks makes me sleepy."

I must have kept up phrases like that for at least ten minutes. I felt more and more sleepy. Finally I drifted off and slept well the rest of the night.

The next morning, I could not recall any trucks. The rest of my family, though, were complaining about the noisy trucks, so it must have been that they kept going by. I felt sorry I didn't teach them what I was doing, but I was grateful and pleased at my response.

You can desensitize yourself to all sorts of things. If I were listening to trucks again, I would have to recall my work and reinforce it. Such things don't last unless we continue to practice them. But you can feel calm and relaxed around things that typically would bother you.

Appendix 2
Breathing Exercises for Calm and Peace

Breathing and heart-focused meditations are traditional ways of achieving calm and peace. Generally you will practice these twice a day, for ten minutes each time, if you want a satisfactory response. You can try them all, or just try one, and stick with it.

If your attention wavers (and it will, I can bet on that!), you just say to yourself, "That is just thinking, thinking." and return to your meditation. Such a practice will help you both physically and mentally.

The lobes exercise: Your lungs are made of three lobes, a top, middle and a bottom lobe. (Well, the right side, anyway. On the left side, the heart occupies the space for the middle lobe.) The chest muscles inflate the top and middle, and the diaphragm muscle, a sheet like muscle between your lungs and your stomach, inflates the bottom lobe.

People with too much anger or fear often breathe only with the tops of their lungs. Using the diaphragm muscle helps you quiet your body.

Fill the bottom third of your lungs first, then the top two thirds. Then breathe out slowly and completely.

Imagine that you fill the bottom and then when you exhale, you blow out the top, then the middle and bottom.

A variation: Exercise 2: Count the number of seconds that you breathe in, and then count the number of seconds you breathe out. Try to breathe in to a count of three and out to the count of 9 or 12.

Another variation: Exercise 3: Count the number of breaths. Count them in sets of four, and change the first number with each new set. So:

    1, 2, 3, 4   (First set)

    2, 2, 3, 4,   (Second set)

    3, 2, 3, 4

    4, 2, 3, 4

Count to sixty, so on that set it is:

    60, 2, 3, 4

Then count back to one.

Likely Effects

This morning as I was working on this chapter, I took my blood pressure. The reading was 128/83, pulse 57. After my "lobes" breathing exercise (counting to 3 on the in-breath, and 9 on the out-breath) for less than five minutes, the reading was 113/74, pulse 55. You can generally expect a drop in blood pressure and in pulse rate.

Psychologically, I feel centered and focused afterwards. Most people tell me they feel more peaceful and centered. Your capacity for original thought will generally increase.

When I can, I will spend twenty minutes during my lunch hour, either doing breathing or autogenic training. I am much more alert and creative through the afternoon when I do that. Some patients can even tell if I have done my meditation!

Wouldn't you like to be at your best?

Appendix 3
Rate your Depression.
CES-D
Copyright Center for Epidemiological Studies.
Reprinted by Permission.

This inventory asks you to describe how you have felt *over the past week*. For each set of answers, circle the number next to the description that best describes you. **During the past week:**

1. I was bothered by things that usually don't bother me.
0 Rarely or none of the time (less than 1 day).
1 Some or a little of the time (1 - 2 days).
2 Occasionally or a moderate amount of the time (3 - 4 days).
3 Most of the time (5 - 7 days).

2. I did not feel like eating; my appetite was poor.
0 Rarely or none of the time (less than 1 day).
1 Some or a little of the time (1 - 2 days).
2 Occasionally or a moderate amount of the time (3 - 4 days).
3 Most of the time (5 - 7 days).

3. I felt I could not shake off the blues even with help from my family and friends.
0 Rarely or none of the time (less than 1 day).
1 Some or a little of the time (1 - 2 days).
2 Occasionally or a moderate amount of the time (3 - 4 days).
3 Most of the time (5 - 7 days).

4. I felt I was just as good as other people.

3 Rarely or none of the time (less than 1 day).
2 Some or a little of the time (1 - 2 days).
1 Occasionally or a moderate amount of the time (3 - 4 days).
0 Most of the time (5 - 7 days).

5. I had trouble keeping my mind on what I was doing.
0 Rarely or none of the time (less than 1 day).
1 Some or a little of the time (1 - 2 days).
2 Occasionally or a moderate amount of the time (3 - 4 days).
3 Most of the time (5 - 7 days).

6. I felt depressed.
0 Rarely or none of the time (less than 1 day).
1 Some or a little of the time (1 - 2 days).
2 Occasionally or a moderate amount of the time (3 - 4 days).
3 Most of the time (5 - 7 days).

7. I felt that everything I did was an effort.
0 Rarely or none of the time (less than 1 day).
1 Some or a little of the time (1 - 2 days).
2 Occasionally or a moderate amount of the time (3 - 4 days).
3 Most of the time (5 - 7 days).

8. I felt hopeful about the future.
3 Rarely or none of the time (less than 1 day).
2 Some or a little of the time (1 - 2 days).
1 Occasionally or a moderate amount of the time (3 - 4 days).
0 Most of the time (5 - 7 days).
9. I thought my life had been a failure.

0 Rarely or none of the time (less than 1 day).
1 Some or a little of the time (1 - 2 days).
2 Occasionally or a moderate amount of the time (3 - 4 days).
3 Most of the time (5 - 7 days).

10. I felt fearful.
0 Rarely or none of the time (less than 1 day).
1 Some or a little of the time (1 - 2 days).
2 Occasionally or a moderate amount of the time (3 - 4 days).
3 Most of the time (5 - 7 days).

11. My sleep was restless.
0 Rarely or none of the time (less than 1 day).
1 Some or a little of the time (1 - 2 days).
2 Occasionally or a moderate amount of the time (3 - 4 days).
3 Most of the time (5 - 7 days).

12. I was happy.
3 Rarely or none of the time (less than 1 day).
2 Some or a little of the time (1 - 2 days).
1 Occasionally or a moderate amount of the time (3 - 4 days).
0 Most of the time (5 - 7 days).

13. I talked less than usual.
0 Rarely or none of the time (less than 1 day).
1 Some or a little of the time (1 - 2 days).
2 Occasionally or a moderate amount of the time (3 - 4 days).
3 Most of the time (5 - 7 days).
14. I felt lonely

0 Rarely or none of the time (less than 1 day).
1 Some or a little of the time (1 - 2 days).
2 Occasionally or a moderate amount of the time (3 - 4 days).
3 Most of the time (5 - 7 days).

15. People were unfriendly
0 Rarely or none of the time (less than 1 day).
1 Some or a little of the time (1 - 2 days).
2 Occasionally or a moderate amount of the time (3 - 4 days).
3 Most of the time (5 - 7 days).

16. I enjoyed life.
3 Rarely or none of the time (less than 1 day).
2 Some or a little of the time (1 - 2 days).
1 Occasionally or a moderate amount of the time (3 - 4 days).
0 Most of the time (5 - 7 days).

17. I had crying spells
0 Rarely or none of the time (less than 1 day).
1 Some or a little of the time (1 - 2 days).
2 Occasionally or a moderate amount of the time (3 - 4 days).
3 Most of the time (5 - 7 days).

18. I felt sad
0 Rarely or none of the time (less than 1 day).
1 Some or a little of the time (1 - 2 days).
2 Occasionally or a moderate amount of the time (3 - 4 days).
3 Most of the time (5 - 7 days).

19 I felt that people dislike me
0 *Rarely or none of the time (less than 1 day).*
1 *Some or a little of the time (1 - 2 days).*
2 *Occasionally or a moderate amount of the time (3 - 4 days).*
3 *Most of the time (5 - 7 days).*

20. I could not get "going"
0 *Rarely or none of the time (less than 1 day).*
1 *Some or a little of the time (1 - 2 days).*
2 *Occasionally or a moderate amount of the time (3 - 4 days).*
3 *Most of the time (5 - 7 days).*

Now sum up your scores. Turn to the next page and see where you score on this depression inventory.

Interpretation of CES-D scores: Add up the number values of the items you circled. These values may change from week to week, and you certainly might want to take the inventory after you have been working on the book's homework assignments, so you can see if you are progressing. Here is what your score means:

0 - 9: Probably not depressed.

10 - 17: Mildly depressed

18 - 27: Moderately depressed

28 - 60 Severely depressed.

Generally if you are around 16 or 17 and upwards, you really ought to seek some help for your mental state. See a psychologist if you want to learn how to deal with your feelings better; see your medical doctor for a prescription if you prefer using medication. Or see them both!

Irritability can be a symptom of depression. If you are depressed, and you are also angry and irritable, you could benefit from curing that irritability and replacing it with optimism, hope, and gratitude. This book has given some hints. You may need more help and so you'd benefit from a therapist.

I am not terribly impressed with medications. They clearly help some people. So does therapy. The medication is less trouble, but successful therapy lasts much longer.

Take your pick. Or combine them. That works better than either alone.

Suggested Readings

Marcus Buckingham & Don Clifton: *Now, Discover Your Strengths.*

Doc Lew Childre & Howard Martin: *The HeartMath Solution: The Institute of HeartMath's Revolutionary Program for Engaging the Power of the Heart's Intelligence*

Thich Nhat Hanh: *Anger: Wisdom for cooling the flames.*

John Lund *How to Hug a Porcupine.*

David Myers *The Pursuit of Happiness.*

George Pransky: *Divorce is not the Answer: A Change of Heart will Change Your Marriage.*

Martin E. P. Seligman, *Authentic Happiness.*

Carol Tavris: *Anger, The Misunderstood Emotion*

Hendrie Davis Weisinger : *Anger at Work/Learning the Art of Anger Management on the Job*

You can easily find these books through any good bookstore. I encourage you to patronize your local independent bookstores, if you can. Chain bookstores don't need your support. Independent booksellers will appreciate it much more.

Many bookstores can find used copies of books for you. If your local bookseller doesn't have used books, try:

www.abebooks.com

This site links independent booksellers all around the country and provides an excellent search service.

This book was created with Word Perfect 9.0 and revised with Word Perfect 13 (or, X3). The *reveal codes* feature alone makes it indispensable. The newest version will also open PDF files. For more information about Word Perfect, see www.corel.com.

Positive psychology is a way of helping people through increasing resiliency and happiness. To learn how to do that in organizations, see my website at www.solution-consulting.com

Every book contains mistakes. To send me notes about this book, corrections of mistakes, or corrections to my ideas, email me at: DrJ@DrLynnJohnson.com

This is a pretty good book, isn't it? I had tons of help, from my family, from my patients, from executive coaching clients. Would you like to help me with the next edition? Email me comments and examples of how the book helped you, and when this printing is all sold out, I may put your story into the next edition. Obviously your name will be changed, but it will still be your story. Let's work together to make the world more free of anger.

If you want to share your story, send it in an email. Don't put it as an attachment but right into the body. Include an address and telephone number for yourself. If I use the story, I will contact you about a release so I can print it. DrJ@DrLynnJohnson.com